Knowing Your Bible

VOLUME 1

An Introductory Survey for
the Everyday Christian

Knowing Your Bible

VOLUME 1

An Introductory Survey for the Everyday Christian

edited by

Calvin L. Smith
David L. Williams

King's Divinity Press
Broadstairs, Kent (United Kingdom)

ISBN-13: 978-0-9562006-4-8

Unless otherwise indicated, all Scripture quotations are from The Holy Bible, English Standard Version, published by HarperCollins © 2001 by Crossway Bibles, a division of Good News Publishers. Used by permission. All rights reserved.

Quotations designated (NET) are from the NET Bible® copyright ©1996-2016 by Biblical Studies Press, L.L.C. http://netbible.com All rights reserved.

Scripture quotations taken from the Amplified® Bible (AMP), Copyright © 2015 by The Lockman Foundation. Used by permission. www.Lockman.org

Edited and typeset by King's Divinity Press
Printed and bound in the United Kingdom by Print on Demand
9 Culley Court, Bakewell Rd, Orton Southgate
Peterborough PE2 6XD

CONTENTS

Introduction

For the Christian the Bible represents his/her central basis of faith. What he/she believes, everything he/she knows about God—His eternal plan, His will for their lives, Christian theology and doctrine—is based upon one's knowledge and understanding of the Bible and how God reveals Himself through His word. Clearly, then, the more the believer knows and understands the Bible, the more effective he or she is as a Christian.

Knowing Your Bible: An Introductory Survey for the Everyday Christian is the first of a series of Knowing Your Bible volumes designed to equip the everyday Christian with a comprehensive and detailed knowledge and understanding of the Christian Scriptures. The series explores the Bible's origins, history, content, interpretation, theology and application, enabling readers to apply Scripture in their lives and ministries, together with communicating that knowledge and understanding effectively.

This first volume serves as the set introductory text to King's Evangelical Divinity School's successful eight-module Knowing Your Bible course series, available for study online (for further information and to enrol visit the King's website at www.kingsdivinity.org). However, this book is also designed as a stand-alone study book for the everyday Christian, whether or not they are enrolled on the Knowing Your Bible course.

This first volume provides readers with an introductory survey of the nature, origins and transmission of the Bible, history and worlds of the Old and New Testaments, an introduction to biblical interpretation, Christian doctrine and historically controversial issues, and finally, biblical prophecy. It is written in a straightforward and accessible style by contributors tutoring at King's.

In chapter one David Williams introduces the Bible,

discussing the difference between general and special revelation and the nature of biblical inspiration. This chapter on the nature of the Bible sets the scene for that which follows. In chapter two Donna Orr provides a survey of the Old Testament and its world, demonstrating why it is essential for Christians to study this large section of Scripture and how to avoid some of the potential pitfalls of Old Testament interpretation and application. Likewise, in chapter three, Matt Wong introduces the world of the New Testament, permitting readers to consider how to go about applying timeless yet historically conditioned Scripture to their lives, thus introducing the challenge of hermeneutics.

Walter Lamberti takes up this challenge in the next chapter, offering an up-to-date survey of prominent approaches to biblical interpretation, thus providing readers with an understanding of the topic of hermeneutics and the tools to commence independent study of the Bible texts. In chapter five Anthony Royle takes this hermeneutical discussion a step further, exploring and discussing the Bible's different literary genres, highlighting the types of literature employed by the Bible authors and providing the reader with details of the main distinguishing features of each.

Building upon the earlier chapters, Thomas Fretwell goes on to make the very important case for the necessity of doctrine in the Christian life in chapter six. Here he discusses the topic from both a personal and a church-wide perspective, examining the practical use of doctrine and the tangible benefits accumulated within the lives of believers who take the time to study doctrine. In chapter seven Calvin Smith explores a specific (and polemical) example of Christian doctrine: Biblical prophecy. Often a highly contentious and divisive issue within parts of Evangelicalism, there is a tendency in some circles to downplay or ignore it completely. This chapter, however, highlights the fundamental importance of eschatology in the Church's proclamation, while eschewing and warning against allowing eschatological schemes to become tests of orthodoxy. The chapter concludes by providing the reader with a basic framework of the often bewildering array of views, together with some practical guidance on how to study the subject independently.

Conveniently, this leads to the final chapter of the book and David Williams' treatment of the place of polemics in the Christian life. Traditionally, polemics is that branch of Theology whereby essential controversial topics are discussed and defended, yet this chapter seeks to widen that approach to include discussion of topics that are not necessarily central, core issues to the Christian faith. This essay takes the approach that engagement in any doctrinal discussion requires two essential elements: firstly, the capacity to confidently handle Scripture, and secondly, the capacity to do so with godly love and a humble attitude. The final chapter thus harmonises and brings together the book's various chapters, encouraging those who have read it to have the confidence that their studies afford them the basic awareness to discuss controversial issues facing the contemporary Church.

As the book's editors we have sought to construct a book that the everyday Christian will find helpful, practical and illuminating. With this in mind we have thought carefully about its practical outworking and accessibility, working closely with the knowledgeable contributors to produce a volume that is accessible. We trust and pray the reader will find this volume a valuable addition to their Christian library and would encourage you to look out for the future volumes delving into some of these issues in greater depth.

Finally, if you have enjoyed this volume, please consider enrolling on the Knowing Your Bible online programme at King's Evangelical Divinity School, led by the book's contributors.

Calvin L. Smith and David L. Williams
November, 2016

CHAPTER 1

Nature of the Bible

DAVID L. WILLIAMS

In Matthew 19:4-6 Jesus is asked a difficult question. Although the topic of the question is not relevant for discussion here, the presupposition of His response represents an instructive foundational understanding for both this first chapter and the remainder of this book. His reply assumes a worldview with at least four specific givens: Firstly, there is a God. Secondly, God has spoken. Thirdly, what God has specifically spoken is communicated to mankind via that which may be read. Fourthly, that which may be read should be accepted as authoritative for faith and practice.

To understand these points naturally raises a number of questions central to the topic of the nature of the Bible, for example: How does God reveal Himself to us? How should we understand and differentiate His special revelation (via that which may be read) from His general revelation (via that which may be perceived), available more broadly either in nature or via the human conscience? Introducing and briefly addressing these preliminary questions early in this chapter will naturally lead to further, more focused considerations regarding the nature of the Bible, the Divine inspiration of Scripture, and its authoritative nature for faith and practice. This chapter will, as an introductory survey, briefly touch upon each of these essential elements. By doing so, the aim will be to provide foundational material for further topical study amongst the Biblical texts, and serve as a catalyst for that which follows within this book.

General and Special Revelation

God's revelation of Himself to humanity may be usefully arranged into two distinct categories: general revelation and special revelation. Theologians have developed the former under the descriptive title "Natural Theology". Under this theological category God can be studied through evidence external to the biblical revelation, for example, via study of the natural world, human conscience or even history. Perhaps the greatest exponent of natural theology in church history is Thomas Aquinas, for whom the existence of God, the immortality of the human soul and the supernatural origin of the Catholic Church could all be demonstrated by pure reason (for a brief description of Aquinas' thought see Bray 1996, 152-154).

For the well-known twentieth century Reformed theologian Louis Berkhof, general revelation

> Rests on the basis of creation, is addressed to all intelligent creatures as such, and is therefore accessible to all men, though as the result of sin they are no more able to read and interpret it aright. (1979, 128)

Bruce Demarest explains

> By effable intuition man knows that God exists and that he imposes moral demands on man. Furthermore, equipped with the religious *a priori*, man as a rational being infers from the data of the visible cosmos further characteristics of the Creator, Ruler, and Judge of the universe. (1982, 247)

Three points may be derived from these quotes. Firstly, general revelation is specific in content; that is, it reveals something about God. Secondly, it is available to all men, and thirdly, the revelation is available in a twofold manner; firstly it is available internally via instinct or conscience, and secondly it is available externally via deduction from the evidence of the visible world.

Unquestionably, in writing to the Church in Rome, Paul the Apostle makes this point patently clear in his insightful indictment of mankind (Rom. 1:19 -20). Yet in spite of the clearly perceived invisible attributes of God manifest to all, Paul explains that the problem of human sin darkens the understanding, resulting in an exchange of truth for a lie. Consequently for Karl Barth, both the notion of general revelation and natural theology were of extremely limited value. For him, humans are unable to know God at all, apart from the specific revelation of Jesus Christ, the Word become flesh (see Baillie & Martin 1937, 49). Evidently then, whilst there is a general revelation of God to mankind this is not sufficient, as human sin prevents the unbeliever from arriving at true knowledge of God. Demarest thus concludes:

> We must make a significant addition to our portfolio of divine knowledge. Through Jesus Christ revealed in inspired Scripture, man comes to know God personally in a redemptive relationship. (Ibid, 247).

Although general revelation is the view that God has communicated Himself to all people irrespective of time or geography, special revelation became necessary on account of the fact that mankind had lost the capacity to maintain a relationship with God. In order for redemptive fellowship to occur, a fuller understanding of the nature and character of God is thus required, and this knowledge, of necessity, must go beyond that which is available in general revelation because factoring human sinfulness into the situation it is insufficient to simply know about God. Note then, that the impetus for special revelation has its origin in the restoration of relationship, that is, the primary aim of this revelation was not an expansion of knowledge but a recovery of relationship. Knowledge in the biblical economy is thus a means to an end. Information leads to acquaintance, and a true knowledge of God ushers in the fear of the Lord and consequently to the beginning of true wisdom (Prov. 9:10). Consequently, any truly meaningful analysis of special revelation and the biblical witness must occur under the rubric of God's redemptive revelation to mankind. In short, the believer has the capacity to perceive something of God via Creation, whereas the unbeliever is unable to do so. Millard Erickson confirms, stating:

> The primary result of special revelation is knowledge of God. By this we mean knowledge not only of the person of God, but also of what he has done, of his creation, of the nature and situation of humans, of the relationship between God and humans. It should also be noted that this is real, objective, rational information communicated from God to humanity. (2013,157)

So, is Barth correct in dismissing the value of general revelation? Certainly the limitations of general revelation require a superior revelation, yet Benjamin Warfield, eminent theologian and perhaps the last of the great Professors of Theology at Princeton Theological Seminary, suggests that special revelation is very much built upon the foundation of general revelation (Warfield 1951,75), thus without the former, the latter becomes incomprehensible. By way of general revelation the Psalmist announces, "The heavens declare the glory of God and the sky above proclaims His handiwork. Day to day pours out speech and night to night reveals knowledge" (Ps 19:1-2), yet "the Preacher" of Ecclesiastes reminds us that whilst "He has made everything beautiful in its time. Also he has put eternity in the heart of man, yet so that he cannot find out what God has done from the beginning to the end" (Ecc 3:11). Special revelation is thus the house built upon the necessary foundations of general revelation.

What is the Bible?
To ask "What is the Bible?" would be to raise a question that is seemingly quite easy to answer as one may state that the Bible is the Church's sacred book. Yet the Bible is

not a book in the strictest sense of the word, but more correctly, it is a collection of works and amongst its pages we find a tremendous diversity of material. The Bible contains sixty-six books, written by approximately forty different authors, in three different languages (Hebrew, Aramaic and Greek) on three different continents over a period of approximately one thousand six hundred years.

Chapters four and five of this book will in turn examine in greater detail the nuances of content and methods of interpretation, but suffice it to say here that within the pages of the biblical revelation we will find many different styles of writing such as narrative prose, legal material, poetry, sayings, prophecy, moral maxims and personal correspondence amongst other types. Yet the reader should exercise great caution when slicing and dicing the texts, for to do so can run the risk of misunderstanding one of the Bible's most distinct and characteristic features; that is, with all its undoubted variety there is a fundamental unity to the Bible. Consequently, whatever value may be derived from within the pages of the Bible, these will not be fully realised by simply dipping into the text in search of favourite verses to cite in support of a preferred doctrine, neither will the habit of selecting short texts for devotional reading fully convey the unique character of the Bible to the reader. By contrast, the unity and full message of the Bible is conveyed only to the serious and persistent student of the text, the reader who grapples, over a period of time, with the totality of the material within its covers.

What then is this unifying principle, or principles, for understanding the totality of the Bible? We have already made the point that special revelation is primarily relational in nature, but beyond this there are in fact many additional unifying principles that could be advanced. For the purposes of this chapter we may simplify by stating that within the pages of the Bible we have a collection of varied material that taken together creates a narrative of human life, across several centuries. Chapter two of this book will present a detailed survey of the Old Testament emergence and subsequent history of the Jewish people, the importance of the Old Testament to the Christian and how some real interpretive difficulties may be overcome. Most people are aware, however, that the Bible consists of not one but two main divisions, known widely as the Old Testament and the New Testament. Chapter three of this book will more fully explore the New Testament, teasing out the actual historical context of the New Testament world, and providing several key insights concluding that whilst the context is culture specific, the message is timeless, for all peoples in all places at all times.

In concluding this section then, we can say that the Bible tells no ordinary history but articulates what German theologians call *Heilsgeschichte,* the "salvation history" of a redeemed people. If the Bible is God's special revelation to mankind, a book that articulates the salvation history of a particular, redeemed people that must correctly be read and studied under the rubric of God's redemptive revelation, then it is incumbent upon us to enquire not just into the contents but also into the inspiration and authoritative nature of the Bible and how the Bible functions in the normative process of establishing God's redemptive plan in the lives of His people.

The *Locus Classicus*
The pages of the Bible make serious claim to divine inspiration, as demonstrated by continuous use of authoritative expressions such as 'Yahweh says'. This phrase and its various derivatives occur "more than 2,000 times" (Bigalke 2010, 5) in the Old Testament alone, and throughout the pages of the Bible there is a presumption of divine authorship. Thus the biblical authors "conveyed - without ambiguity- that they did not speak on their own, but God revealed to them a special message to record" (ibid).

Paul's statement in 2 Tim 3:16 is the *locus classicus* for any discussion of the inspiration of the biblical texts. There are a variety of interpretational issues to resolve in this verse: Firstly, what is the meaning of γραφή (*graphē*)? Does it refer to mere writings in the general sense or more specifically to Scripture? And if the latter, is the primary reference to just the Old Testament or to both the Old and the New Testaments? Further, should reference be limited to the original autographs or does it include later copies? (On this latter point see G L Bahnsen, 1973, 47 and E W Goodrick 1982, 481-483.) The term "γραφή" as employed in the New Testament refers to the Old Testament "for that is what the word *graphē* refers to in every single one of its fifty-one occurrences in the New Testament" (Grudem, 1994, 74). Yet there are two places where the term appears to hint at the teachings of Jesus and Paul, and thus could refer to parts of the New Testament. In 1 Tim 5:18, Paul quotes the Old Testament text prohibiting the muzzling of an ox (Deut. 25:4) and follows this with the point that "the worker deserves his wages". The latter is a verbatim quote from Luke 10:7, which Paul here appears to equate with scripture. Likewise in 2 Peter 3:16, Peter bemoans those who distort Paul's letters "as they do the other scriptures (γραφή)". Peter is apparently placing Paul's writings alongside sacred scripture. We may conclude that whilst the New Testament authors consistently employ *graphē* with explicit reference to the Old Testament, implicit reference may also be taken to those portions of the New Testament available at the time of writing. The implication is that the term can be attributed to the entire Bible.

A further interpretive issue within 2 Timothy 3:16 arises over the precise grammatical relationship of θεόπνευστος (*theópneustos* – lit. God inspired) to "γραφή" (scriptures); that is, should the phrase be rendered as "all God inspired scripture" (attributive) or as "all scripture is inspired by God" (predicate)? Wayne House suggests that both are "grammatically permissible", with the solution ultimately determined by context (1980, 57). Certainly whilst the former is syntactically possible it does appear quite convoluted, and the latter is perhaps a more natural reading of the Greek text. Thus Goodrick arrives at the translation "All scripture is God breathed" (1982, 483). Likewise, the New English Translation (NET) Bible renders

11

the text accurately as "every scripture is inspired by God and useful for teaching…" This does seem to be the likeliest English rendering of the Greek phrase.

How Are The Scriptures Inspired?

What, precisely, is meant by the term inspiration? In what sense are the biblical texts inspired? There has been much debate on this topic generally, and it will be helpful to briefly survey a few of the more prominent positions. Whilst running the risk of the accusation of oversimplification, we can state that there are three common approaches to this question, although some further subtle variations of approach do occur.

One popular position is to state that the Bible functions as the word of God by a process of divine dictation, whereby, when stated without nuance, the human authors became little more than God's secretaries. According to this theory, God told the biblical authors precisely what to write. A prime example of this view is that

> The bible is none other than the voice of Him that sitteth upon the throne. Every book of it, every chapter of it, every verse of it, every word of it, every syllable of it, every letter of it, is the direct utterance of the Most High. The Bible is none other than the Word of God, not some part of it more, some part of it less, but all alike the utterance of Him who sitteth upon the throne, unerring, supreme. (John Burgon, cited in Abba 1958, 64)

Although this dictation theory was once popular it generally attracts little support from modern biblical scholars. The essential problem with this theory is that it pays little heed to some of the central features of the biblical text. Certainly there are portions of the Bible in which a biblical author makes the categorical and unequivocal claim of having received a direct revelation from God that was subsequently written down. For example, the apostle John encountered the risen Jesus on the Isle of Patmos and was told specifically to write letters to the seven churches (Revelation 2:8, 12, 18, 3:1, 7,14). This is a clear example of God dictating Scripture to the human author.

By contrast, there are many other passages that are seemingly constructed in a different manner. A classic example is in the introduction to the third gospel, where Luke informs Theophilus that his intention is to write an orderly account on the basis of the many who had previously "undertaken to compile a narrative" (Lk 1:1-4). Analysis of Luke's gospel and his subsequent volume, the Acts of the Apostles, appears to bear out the notion that Luke researched and made much use of the work of others in assembling his own accounts. Likewise, there are situations where biblical authors quote secular sources, for example in Paul's appearance at the Areopagus, it is clear that he quotes "some of your own poets", likely Epimenides and Aratus (Acts 17:28). It is certainly problematic to imagine God dictating Greek secular sources to Luke.

And so arises a second theory, which may be termed the "intuition" theory (Erickson 2013,174), whereby the Bible is seen to be inspired in much the same way that human genius is often described, such as in the composition of one of Mozart's symphonies or a Shakespearean play. Inspiration, in this sense, is little more than the employment of a natural human talent, by which the biblical authors were gifted with superior religious erudition in their capacities to compose sacred literature. Consequently the texts are no more inspired than any other great work of human literature, that is, the Bible is a human book. If the texts are deemed to be the word of God, then it is only in the sense that certain passages convey either a powerful moral force or the self-revealing activity of God. This view insists that "divine truth is not located in an ancient book but in the on-going work of the Spirit in the community, as discerned by critical, rational judgement" (Pinnock 1977, 53). James Packer points out

13

that the legacy of such a position is the "axiom that certainly some biblical teaching and perhaps all, is not revealed truth; biblical affirmations, therefore should not be received except as confirmed by reason"(1999, 67-68). Man and his enlightened rationale now become the focal point of all things theological and the need to submit oneself to the reproving judgements of scripture disappear in what Packer calls "an unwarrantable confidence in the power of the unaided human mind to work out religious truth for itself" (Ibid., 67). It therefore becomes the duty of the Bible student to accept or reject portions of the text in such a manner that becomes impossible to justify, and then to impose an interpretation of his own subjective making. The situation is neatly summed up by a satirical epigram

> "Hic liber est in quo quareit sua dogmata unique ;Invenit et pariter dogmata unique sua" - "This is the book where everyone seeks his own opinion; this is the book where still everyone finds what he seeks". (cited in Dodd 1946, 22)

Yet it is important to state that whilst this view fails to account for the divine element within the biblical texts, as seen in the example of the risen Lord Jesus dictating to John the letters to the seven churches in Revelation, we would do well to appreciate that this position does place a very needed emphasis upon the human authorship of the Bible, and its role as literature. Any complete view of the Bible will fully account for the human role in the composition of the text. Yet as Packer elsewhere points out, the "intuition" theory is fundamentally a contradiction of the clear statement of Scripture (2 Tim. 3:16), namely, that every part of Scripture has a divine origin (1958, 80)

A third view, as exemplified by theologian Karl Barth, is that the Bible becomes the word of God under the inspiration of the Holy Spirit, as God speaks to us today. Barth's neo-orthodoxy, as the name suggests, sought a return from the liberalism of the "Intuition" view to the salvation-centred orthodoxy of the Reformation, yet he wished to do so without returning to belief in mechanical inspiration of the Bible. Barth's essential thesis is that the Bible is the vessel by which the occasion of revelation reoccurs; that is, God is able to disclose himself to a sinful world via a human book, the Bible. Thus for Barth, the prime issue in biblical inspiration is not to be seen in the composition of the texts as they were originally written, but in its present day functionality in the lives of God's people. He contends that

> The statement, "The Bible is God's Word," is a confession of faith, a statement made by faith that hears God Himself speak in the human word of the Bible... The Bible therefore becomes God's Word in this event ... It does not become God's Word because we accord it faith, but of course, because it becomes revelation for us. (Barth 1936, 123-124)

Consequently, the Bible is God's inspired word only "so far as God lets it be His word, so far as God speaks through it" (Ibid). For Barth, this erring human Bible, which may become God's word, is also the final authority for man's religious life and becomes the standard for all right thinking, teaching and behaving in spite of the errors it contains. One may state that such a view of inspiration is based upon a false antithesis and a deficient exegesis of the term θεόπνευστος (theopneustos) in 2 Tim 3:16. Yet Barth's innovative approach to the functioning of the Bible in the life of the contemporary believer can be welcomed and cautiously embraced, if with some qualification. Conversely, there is some danger here too, for as Colin Brown has stated

> It is impossible to maintain high doctrines of revelation and inspiration without at the same time being willing to defend in detail the veracity and historicity of the biblical writers. (1999,146)

It is precisely here that Barth fails us, for whilst he affirmed that the biblical authors could err in their writings, (although he is painfully slow to point to any specific instances of what he considers to be mistaken); in practice he appears to demonstrate great trust in the Bible to reveal Christ.

All of these theories of inspiration have something of value to offer us, and are only necessarily in conflict when held in isolation. We have seen that there are elements of both divine dictation and human qualities within the Bible, whilst to Barth's great credit he laid continuous emphasis upon the sovereignty and lordship of God, man's incapacity on account of sin to seek and find God, and on the actuality of our communion with God, through Christ via the word that He speaks to us; that is, the functioning of the Bible as conveying the reality of Christ to man.

Perhaps then, it is possible to suggest a more nuanced theory of the inspiration of the Bible. We may term this a dynamic theory, which emphasises equally the combination of divine and human strands weaved into the process of inspiration and composition of the Bible. Thus, from a human perspective we are able to describe its composition in terms of varied genre and literary processes that account for the collection of information from various witnesses and sources. Likewise, from a divine perspective it is possible to postulate that God's Spirit was active in controlling the compositional process such that the end result is a scripture "breathed out by God" (Warfield 1951, 245), that is, the composition process of the Bible was under the supervision and control of the Holy Spirit.

Consequently, to acknowledge that the Bible witnesses to the acts of God in history, via genuinely human language conventions and processes, and that the texts have a dynamic impact in the life of the contemporary believer as he encounters, by faith, the words on the page does not necessitate a denial that God has sovereignly superintended the entire process such that the text of the Bible contains precisely what He wanted.

The Bible, by this reckoning can be described as the word of God composed in the word of man. The Bible is God's word yet it did not descend from Heaven, fully composed. It is God's word simply because He inspired it to be written as a witness to Himself. The Bible is God's word because it has its origin in God. Yet the Bible is the word of man, because it is composed of human words, for all words are human, and the Bible thus portrays the marks of the human literary conventions and grammatical principles of the times and cultures in which the documents were recorded. Erickson thus concludes,

> Because the Bible has been inspired, we can be confident of having divine instruction. The fact that we did not live when the revelatory events and teachings first came does not leave us spiritually or theologically deprived. We have a sure guide. And we are motivated to study it intensely, since its message is truly God's word to us. (2013, 187)

The Reliability of the Bible

Confidence in the inspired nature of the Bible implies a logical corollary for the dependability of the text; that is the question of the inerrancy and authority of the biblical texts. Stated briefly, the concept of biblical inerrancy is the "doctrine that the Bible is fully truthful in all its teachings" (Erickson 2013, 188). By contrast, a Bible that contains demonstrable errors would undermine the credibility of any claim to a thorough and dependable reliability of the texts. This is a vital concern, and one that perhaps culminates the doctrine of Scripture. It is important that the reader grasps precisely what is meant by the term, and how it is applied in connection to Scripture, as any discussion of the topic remains central to exegetical and hermeneutical issues. The doctrine of inerrancy, as customarily formulated, postulates that the necessary character of the truth claims of the Bible is guaranteed upon the God whose word it is, that is, if God is by His nature inerrant, then it follows that His word (if that is what the Bible truly is) must by necessity be inerrant also. The Bible is thus wholly true on account of the fact that its primary author, God, is all knowing and reliable.

This understanding opens a further consideration, namely the question of the perpetual and unchanging nature of the truths of Scripture. Scripture may have been correct at one point in time, as written by the original authors, but it does not necessarily follow that momentary truth implies perpetual truth. For example, a telephone directory may be momentarily true, but it is not likely to be perpetually true, as people move home and change their telephone numbers. Indeed no such guarantee is ever implied with any telephone directory publication. Consequently any concept of a perpetually inerrant text must imply more than just being true at any single given point in time. Beyond this, arises a further consideration; a text may be inerrant yet still mislead the reader, if such a one approaches said text with incorrect beliefs or assumptions. For example, a visitor to Holland attempting to navigate a course through Amsterdam whilst holding a map of Rotterdam would find his map mislead him in quite spectacular fashion. The map of Rotterdam would remain thoroughly accurate, inerrant even, yet reader false presupposition has on this occasion rendered the map thoroughly errant in use.

The Christian, by faith, holds that the Bible is true on the first occasion because the ultimate author is God. It therefore remains true on each subsequent reading, again not on account of random coincidence, but because of the nature and character of its divine author, who knows all things. Consequently, each and every time the Bible is consulted, it will, if approached correctly, with great exegetical precision, yield unfailing truth, useful for all manner of corrective purposes. This is a thorough undergirding of the *locus classicus* principles of 2 Tim 3:16, God's "breathing out" of His authoritative word, from himself through his appointed human agents, such that the expression of Scripture is both His own word yet bearing the hallmark and conventions of human language.

Conclusion

This chapter commenced with the assertion that Jesus' employment of Scripture assumed a fourfold worldview through which God communicates via that which may be read. A further implication is that if the words in the Bible are God's words, then they carry His authority and so failure to believe or obey any word in Scripture is tantamount to failing to believe or obey God Himself. Yet, it is clear that God's self-disclosure is not limited to the words of Scripture alone, but that He has also revealed Himself via broader categories. Theologians have termed this broader disclosure "General Revelation", whereby God's "invisible attributes, namely his eternal power and divine nature have been clearly perceived, ever since the creation of the world, in the things that have been made" (Rom 1:20). The entrance of sin darkened the collective human understanding, resulting in an "exchange of truth for a lie" (Rom 1:25) with the outcome that general revelation became extremely limited in value. Special revelation, therefore, became necessary on account of the fact that mankind had lost the capacity to maintain a relationship with God. Special revelation is thus the house built upon the necessary foundations of general revelation.

The next section asked the question "What is the Bible?" The answer is that it is a compendium of sixty-six books written over an extended period and incorporates a range of differing literary genres. The Bible is also a book concerned with *Heilsgeschichte,* the salvation history of a redeemed people, and thus represents God's "special revelation" of Himself to His people. The Bible should therefore be studied under the rubric of God's redemptive purposes for mankind.

The Bible makes some serious internal claims to being God's word and so the next section concentrated on a discussion of two issues. Consideration of the *locus classicus* of 2 Timothy 3:16, was followed by an extended survey of three popular, but polarised, positions on the nature of biblical inspiration. The conclusion drawn is that the three theories surveyed remain in conflict only when viewed in isolation, thus a further nuanced position was proposed, whereby it is acknowledged that the Bible clearly contains elements that fit both the divine dictation and human compositional categories. Likewise, with Barth, it is acknowledged that via contemporary Divine encounters the Bible continues to "become God's word" in the life of His people as they study it. We termed this position the "dynamic theory" of inspiration by which we understand that God has so superintended the process of composition that the Bible contains precisely that which He intended, yet the text is also composed via genuinely human language conventions and processes. This conclusion should encourage the serious student of Scripture to appreciate and take full account of differing literary types and genres, historical background, language studies and the like whilst noting and submitting to the authoritative nature of a thoroughly dependable set of Christian Scriptures. The following chapters in this book will thus be devoted to assisting the Bible student in this pursuit.

References

Abba, R. (1958), *The Nature And Authority Of The Bible.* London: James Clarke & Co. Ltd.

Bahnsen, G. L. (1973), "Autographs, Amanuensis and Restricted Inspiration" in *Evangelical Quarterly 45* (2), 100-110.

Barth, K. (1936), *Church Dogmatics I/1.* Vol. 1. (G. Thomson, Trans.) Edinburgh: T&T Clark.

Barth, K. (1937), *Revelation.* (J. Baillie, & H. Martin, Eds.) New York: Macmillan.

Berkhof, L. (1979), *Introduction to Systematic Theology.* Grand Rapids, MI: Baker Book House, (Rev. ed.).

Bigalke, R. J. (Aug 2010), "Editorial" in *Journal of Dispensational Theology , 14* (42), 5.

Bray, G. (1996), *Biblical Interpretation: Past & Present.* Downer's Grove, Illinois: InterVarsity Press.

Brown, C. (1998), *Karl Barth And The Christian Message* (2nd ed.). Eugene, OR: Wipf and Stock.

Demarest, B. A. (1982), *General Revelation: Historical Views and Contemporary Issues.* Grand Rapids, MI: Zondervan.

Dodd, C. H. (1968), *The Bible Today.* Cambridge: University Press.

Erickson, M. J. (2013), *Christian Theology* (Third Edition ed.). Grand Rapids, MI: Baker Academic.

Goodrick, E. W. (1982), "Let's Put 2 Timothy 3:16 Back In The Bible" in *Journal of the Evangelical Theological Society 25* (4), 479-487.

Grudem, W. (1994), *Systematic Theology: An Introduction To Biblical Docrtine.* Leicester: Inter-Varsity Press.

House, H. W. (1980), Biblical Inspiration in 2 Timothy 3:16. *Bibliotheca Sacra , 137* (545), 54-61.

Packer, J. I. (1958), *"Fundamentalism" And The Word of God.* Leicester: Inter-Varsity Fellowship.

Packer, J. I. (1999), *Honouring The Written Word Of God.* Carlisle: Paternoster Press.

Pinnock, C. (1977), "Three Views Of The Bible In Contemporary Theology" in J. Rogers, Ed., *Biblical Authority.* Waco, TX: W Publishing Group.

Warfield, B. B. (1951), in B. B. Warfield, & S. G. Craig, eds., *The Inspiration And Authority Of The Bible.* London: Marshall, Morgan & Scott.

CHAPTER 2

A Survey of the Old Testament

DONNA ORR

Neglect of the Old Testament

Tragically today many Christians pay little attention to the Old Testament (hereafter OT). By concentrating all their reading and study in the New Testament (hereafter NT), many Christians are inadvertently imitating the second century heretic, Marcion of Sinope, who rejected the OT in its entirety, as well as the God of Israel, believing him to be a lower and separate entity than the God of the NT. Marcion only recognized eleven books as Scripture: a mutilated Gospel of Luke[1] and ten of Paul's epistles (Metzger 1989, 91-92). However, it is hoped that by the end of this chapter the reader will be encouraged to re-visit the OT, once it is established *why* it is important to study the OT, *how* to avoid some of the pitfalls of OT interpretation and application, and *what* material the OT actually contains.

Importance of the Old Testament

The United Bible Societies' *Greek New Testament* (4ᵗʰ rev. ed., 1993) lists 343 OT quotations in the NT, as well as no fewer than 2,309 allusions[2] and verbal parallels (cited in Motyer

---

[1] Church Fathers, such as Tertullian, and many modern scholars agree that Marcion edited the Gospel of Luke to suit his own theology (Tertullian, *Adversus Marcionem*, 4.6). Marcion omitted the accounts of the nativity, baptism and temptation of Jesus, amongst others.

[2] These are indirect references to the Old Testament, e.g. Matthew 16:4. The "sign of Jonah", mentioned here, refers back to Jonah 1:17, where

1996). Additionally, with the exception of Philemon and 2ⁿᵈ and 3ʳᵈ John, every NT writing contains quotations from or allusions to the OT (Evans 2004, 130). Christians often forget the interdependence of the two Testaments and the continuity of the New with the Old. Greidanus (1999, 48) has pointed out, "Redemptive history is the mighty river that runs from the old covenant to the new and holds the two together." Greidanus understands that there is progression in this history, but it is still a *single* redemptive history (ibid.). The OT needs the NT and the NT needs the OT to be properly interpreted and understood. For instance, the epistle to the Hebrews would be incomprehensible without the historical background of the OT.

Likewise, when we read in Galatians 3:29 that we are "Abraham's offspring" and "heirs according to promise" then we are compelled to turn to Genesis to gain an understanding of these terms. As explained in Houdman (2014, 159), "the New Testament is only completely understood when it is seen as being a fulfilment of the events, characters, laws, sacrificial system, covenants and promises of the Old Testament". In fact, if we only had the NT, we would be puzzled as to why the Jews were looking for a Messiah and we would not be able to identify Jesus of Nazareth as this Messiah. However, the many detailed prophecies that are given concerning Him in the OT make this identification possible, for example, His birth place (Mic 5:2); His manner of death (Ps 22; 69:21); His resurrection (Ps 16:10) and many more details of His ministry (Isa 61:1-2), etc. (ibid.). Therefore, the OT forms a backdrop against which we can understand the NT. The NT is the fulfilment of God's plans, purposes and promises which He gave in the OT. The OT points towards Jesus, and the NT describes His life, death, resurrection, as well as His present ministry in heaven and the importance of these events to mankind. Thus, we can say that all Scripture is thoroughly Christocentric and as such,

---

Jonah is described as being in the belly of the fish three days and nights.

requires careful study and application. Three prominent voices in the NT (Christ, Peter and Paul) reiterate this understanding of the OT. Through their testimony we discover that the OT revolves around the person and work of Jesus Christ - Christ in the shadows, but Christ nonetheless.

Christ's View of the Old Testament

Early in His ministry, when speaking to the Jews after the healing at the pool of Bethesda, Jesus describes the Scriptures (the OT) as "they that bear witness about me" (John 5:39) and specifically that Moses wrote of Him (5:46). On speaking a little later to the Jews, Jesus reminds them that their father, the patriarch Abraham "rejoiced that he would see my day. He saw it and was glad" (John 8:56). Also, when Jesus wanted to establish His deity, He would often refer back to the Old Testament (Matt 22:41-46; John 8:58). At the end of His earthly ministry, as the resurrected Jesus is making his way to Emmaus with two of his followers, Jesus rebukes these two for being slow to believe all that the prophets have spoken regarding His suffering and His entry into His glory (Luke 24:25-26). Then Jesus takes them on a whistle stop tour of the OT through Moses and the Prophets and as He interprets text after text, it is as though He is saying, "There I am, there I am and there I am" (Luke 24:27). Later that same day when Jesus appears to the Eleven and those gathered with them, He specifically mentions the threefold division of the Hebrew Bible: Torah, Nevi'im and Ketuvim (the Law, the Prophets and the Psalms) and how these speak of His person, work and the proclamation of His name to the nations (Luke 24:44-47).

Peter's View of the Old Testament

On the Day of Pentecost as the apostle Peter addresses the gathered crowd, he quotes the words of David from Psalm 16:8-11, and explains that David actually "foresaw and spoke about the resurrection of the Christ" (Acts 2:31). He concludes this Pentecost address by employing Psalm

110:1 to prove that Jesus whom the Jews had crucified was actually "Lord and Christ" (Acts 2:36). Additionally, after healing the lame man at the temple, Peter again addresses a crowd and tells them of the fulfilment in their time of "what God foretold by the mouth of all the prophets, that his Christ would suffer ..." (Acts 3:18). Peter expands further by detailing how these prophets, who included Moses and Samuel, spoke of how God would raise up His special servant, who Peter identifies as Christ (Acts 3:21-26). In his epistle Peter particularly shows how the substance of OT prophecies is essentially Christ and His cross. He records how, by the Spirit, the OT prophets proclaimed Christ's sufferings and resurrection (1 Pet 1:11). The same Spirit who guided them also guided the NT preachers in declaring this good news effectively to Peter's readers (1 Pet 1:12). The prophets were living in the shadows, studying, enquiring about and longing for the things we experience today. They prophesised about the grace that we were to receive (1 Pet 1:10). This should affect the way we read the OT; it should increase our appreciation of what we have.

Paul's View of the Old Testament
Similarly, the apostle Paul, in his defence before Agrippa, testified that he was only reiterating what had been stated by the prophets and Moses that Christ would suffer and rise from the dead, leading to the proclamation of the gospel to both the Jews and Gentiles (Acts 26:22-23). Whilst at the beginning of his epistle to the Romans, Paul explains that the gospel of God concerning the Son was "promised beforehand through his prophets in the holy Scriptures" (Rom 1:2). Later in the same epistle Paul relates how "the Law and the Prophets" are a witness to the revelation of God's righteousness in Christ (Rom 3:21-22). In fact, Paul even states in 1 Corinthians 10:4 that the Rock in the wilderness that provided water for the thirsty saints was Christ Himself! Later Paul tells these same Corinthians that the key to understanding the writings of Moses is through turning to Christ (2 Cor 3:14-16).

Therefore, it is evident that these three prominent voices in the NT are in agreement. The OT is Christian Scripture. Although it recounts the history of the ancient Israelites, the people of God, and God's self-revelation to them, it is in essence pointing throughout to their promised Messiah and Saviour, Jesus Christ.

Interpretative Difficulties of the Old Testament

However, it must be acknowledged that God's revelation did not come to us via the English language or Western culture or even in the twenty-first century, and therefore, it is necessary for those of us today who live in the West to work harder to receive the message clearly. The more familiar we can become with ancient Near Eastern culture, particularly that of Israel during the OT period, the easier the process will be. It is always important to remember that the Bible was not written in a vacuum. It reflects the social and cultural contexts in which its authors lived. It is rooted in history and claims to be a historical document, the record of God's self-revelation to man. As McQuilkin (1992, 67) has said,

> God chose to reveal Himself and His will, not in a catalogue of propositional truths recorded in a celestial language, but to people in history by using human language. Therefore, it is our responsibility to study the Bible as we would any other human communication to determine as accurately as possible what the authors intended us to understand, believe and obey.

In order to do this, consideration must be made of two contexts: the historical and literary contexts. Placing a text in its historical context or setting includes determining the events that led up to the text and what was happening at the time, locally, nationally and internationally. The literary context refers to the material that works with and surrounds the passage under consideration. Words, phrases, sentences and paragraphs have no explicit

27

meaning apart from a specific context. Determining the literary context can involve many layers: analysing a passage within a chapter, within a section of a Biblical book, within a complete book, and within the Scriptures as a whole. It is vital to keep both historical and literary contexts in mind when studying the Old Testament. This can be further complicated by the fact that there can be a difference between when the book was written and the time of the events which the book is recording. Osborne (1991, 19) has stressed the importance of context for ascertaining the meaning of a passage, which he compares to scaffolding. He argues, "Without a strong scaffolding, the edifice of interpretation is bound to collapse" (ibid.). Unfortunately, many Christians, influenced by our postmodern individualistic world, are quick to appropriate verses which do not apply to them. They jump to trying to discover the meaning of a passage for their situation without giving careful consideration to what it meant to the original recipients or, even more importantly, the author's original intention when writing. Often they read the Bible selectively, assuming their needs and desires are authoritative over God's Word, and they wrongly ask, "How can I use the bits I like, to say the things I like?" This is what is known as *eisegesis*, instead of *exegesis* of a text. Therefore, it is helpful to initially acquire a sound background knowledge and understanding of the history, religion, society and literature of the OT and the interrelationships between the various OT books. Once the meaning of a passage to the original readers has been established, then more accurate application can be achieved.

---

[3] Postmodernism is a philosophical and cultural movement, distinguished largely by its rejection of Modernism. It includes the understanding that all truth is relative and, therefore, what is right for one group is not necessarily right or true for everyone. It rejects grand narratives, ways of thinking that seek to provide a definitive, universal truth. It emphasizes the role of the individual; knowledge is interpreted according to the individual's "local" experience.

However, it is important to remember that Biblical history is told with a theological purpose and from a theological vantage point. Therefore, it is both history and theology. Dillard and Longman (1995, 23) maintain "biblical history is not an objective reporting of purely human events. It is an impassioned account of God's acts in history as he works in the world to save his people." Thus, to McCartney and Clayton (2002, 226-27) this means,

> first, we must respect the historical integrity of the texts, and that, second, we must recognize a purpose deeper than telling 'what actually happened' from a human standpoint ... we must ask what the theological *purpose* of the text is and *how* it is relating the history.

Additionally, an appreciation for the diversity of genre within Scripture is also crucial to its interpretation. The books of the Bible represent several genres, or types of literary compositions. McCartney and Clayton (2002, 223) list "worship literature, historical narratives, love poems, prophecies, legal codes, and wisdom literature" as some of the different genres in the OT. It is particularly important to be careful when dealing with OT law and narrative. Fee and Stuart (2003, 167-68) explain that the Israelite civil and ritual laws have not been renewed in the new covenant. They point out that the civil laws only apply to the citizens of ancient Israel and "no one living today is a citizen of ancient Israel" (ibid.). They also demonstrate that the ritual laws have been made obsolete by the once-for-all sacrifice of Christ (ibid.). Regarding narratives, Fee and Stuart (2003, 105-6) also remind us that,

> Narratives are precious to us because they so vividly *demonstrate* God's involvement in the world and *illustrate* his principles and calling. They thus teach us a lot – but what they directly teach us does not systematically include personal ethics.

The purpose of the OT is not to hold up flawless characters whose lives are to be imitated. It will become apparent, after even a cursory reading of the OT, that just because Abraham or King David did something, does not make it always correct. Therefore, Hill and Walton (1991, 4) have explained, "The Old Testament is not a repository of historical role models, dusty hymns, and obscure prophetic sayings, but God's invitation to hear his story."

Seven Historical Eras of the Old Testament

If, as is noted above, it is acknowledged that history is a vehicle through which God has chosen to reveal Himself, then it would be helpful to divide the OT into historical eras in order to determine its contents. As Köstenberger and Patterson (2011, 97) maintain, "An accurate chronology thus provides the interpreter with the necessary framework for interpreting a given Old Testament passage in its historical context."

The book of Genesis, the book of origins or beginnings, covers the first two periods of Biblical history: the Primeval History (chs. 1-11) and the Patriarchal Era (chs. 12-50). However, Marvin Pate et al. (2004, 29) mourn that this division has "resulted in an unfortunate bifurcation of the book ..." They are correct. Certainly, this book is one book, organised around its "elleh toledoth" formulas (meaning "these are the generations"), which appear eleven times (2:4; 5:1; 6:9; 10:1; 11:10; 11:27; 25:12; 25:19; 36:1; 36:9 and 37:2). However, in terms of dating the events contained in the book, this two-fold historical division is helpful. The Primeval History covers the period from the beginning to Abraham (ca. 2000 BC), whilst the Patriarchal Era extends from Abraham to Moses (ca. 2000-1600 BC). In terms of content, Pate et al. (2004, 23) have highlighted an interesting refrain that appears in Genesis, as well as being repeated throughout Israel's history. This is the paradigm of sin-exile-restoration, which emerges as a result of the constant tension between divine will and human responsibility. Thankfully Genesis 3:15 gives us a glimpse of the One who would ultimately conquer Satan and make it possible for mankind to be permanently restored to God through faith in this Messiah.

The events recorded in the remaining books of the Law (Exodus - Deuteronomy) take place during the years ca. 1876-1400 BC (depending on how one dates the Exodus – see Walton's chronological chart, 1994, 99). This is the historical period of the Egyptian Captivity and the Exodus. There are so many uncertainties within this period of Biblical history. How long did the Israelites sojourn in Egypt? In what year did the Exodus occur? What route did the Israelites take as they journeyed from Egypt to Mount Sinai? However, what is certain is that the Exodus was a momentous event in the history of the Israelite people. Fee and Stuart (2003, 163) see it as being one of "three defining narratives" for the Israelites. Having miraculously delivered His people from slavery in Egypt, the presence of God is assured to distinguish His people from all other peoples on earth (Exod 33; 40) and then God reconstitutes them as a people for His name at Mount Sinai (Exod 19 - Num 10:10) (ibid.). Needless to say, they needed direction as to how they were to be God's people, both in their relationships with each other and with God, and that was the purpose of the Law in Israel's history (ibid.). However, as Paul teaches the Galatians, the Law was ultimately a "tutor" or "guardian" designed to reveal man's sinfulness and inadequacy, thus sending him to Christ to find justification by faith (Gal 3:19, 24).

The Conquest and Judges period of Israelite history covers the historical years ca. 1406-1050 BC, and a record of this time is found in the Biblical books of Joshua, Judges and Ruth in which is recounted the commissioning of Joshua right through to the emergence of Samuel, the priest, prophet and judge. As the date of the Exodus is debated, obviously the date of the Conquest will also be uncertain. The "early date" for the Conquest places it ca. 1400 BC, whilst the "late date" sets it ca. 1220 BC. Lasor, Hubbard and Bush (1996, p. 152) argue that one of the major concerns of Joshua is that of rest "from the pangs of slavery, the hardships of the wilderness, and the rigors of war (e.g., 1:13; 11:23)." This is echoed in Judges when the land has rest at the end of each repeated cycle of idolatry, oppression from a foreign nation, the people crying out to Yahweh, and His raising up of a deliverer, who ultimately defeats the oppressor. This basic truth of a rest for the people of God "develops into a rich doctrine of future hope and blessing ... with a heavenly place of rest from the rigors of the earthly pilgrimage. Jesus, the New Joshua, offered such rest to all who come to him (Matt 11:28)" (ibid.).

As Israel demands a king, the nation could not have known what lay ahead in both the time of the United Monarchy (ca. 1050-931 BC) and the Divided Monarchy (ca. 931-586 BC). This period is documented in the historical books of 1 and 2 Samuel, 1 and 2 Kings, and 1 and 2 Chronicles. The years of the United Monarchy incorporate the reigns of Saul, David and Solomon and are sometimes known as "Israel's Golden Age", if value is measured in terms of politics and economics (La Sor, Hubbard and Bush 1996, 182). The inspiring psalmody and wisdom literature of such Biblical books as Psalms, Proverbs, Ecclesiastes and Song of Songs were also written within this period, and possibly Job (although its setting appears to be the Patriarchal Era ca. 2000 BC). When the kingdom is divided into Israel and Judah, it is only Judah that is ruled by the descendants of David. Although there is an attempt by a few of Judah's kings (Asa, Josiah and Hezekiah) to return the people to a true worship of Yahweh, many of David's descendants continue to lead Judah into appalling apostasy. Even the attempts to call Israel and Judah back to Yahweh by the prophets, such as Elijah, Elisha, Isaiah, Jeremiah, Hosea, Joel, Amos, Micah, Habakkuk and Zephaniah, are to no avail. Samaria in the Northern Kingdom falls to Assyria in 722 BC and its population is deported, whilst Judah is captured by the Babylonians in 586 BC. The theological point that emerges from this period, even when reading the narrative of the Israelite king par excellence, King David, is "the sober reality that David is not the ultimate deliverer" (Pate et al.

2004, 63). A more qualified Messiah is still to come, the Son of David and King of Kings, Jesus Christ.

The Babylonian Exile and Resettlement in Judah spans the years ca. 586-400 BC. Psalm 137 captures the extent of the sorrow caused by this captivity. As the Exile had taken place in three stages (605, 597 and 586 BC) so the Resettlement also takes place in three stages (538 BC led by Sheshbazzar; 458 BC led by Ezra; and 445 BC led by Nehemiah). Ezekiel, Daniel, Haggai, Zechariah and Malachi are the writing prophets who speak into the situation of that time. Although, the last word of Malachi's prophecy is "curse", the promise of an Elijah, a forerunner yet to come, offers hope that a curse will not be God's last word. In Jesus, God's grace and not His curse is the final word (Rev 22:21).

Conclusion
In this chapter, in view of the OT's thoroughly Christocentric nature, the importance to the Christian of studying the OT has been established. This Christocentric emphasis is echoed by three prominent voices in the NT: Jesus, Peter and Paul. However, it has also been acknowledged that, because of differences in language, culture and historical era, it is difficult to interpret and apply the OT Scripture today, especially for those in the West. Some of the common pitfalls in this respect have been identified and ways to avoid them have been considered. Finally, as God's revelation is rooted in the context of history, the OT has been divided into seven historical eras and an attempt has been made to summarise its contents. It is hoped this will encourage the reader to revisit the OT. The OT's value cannot be overestimated. As Terence Noble (2010, 1529) sums it up,

> ... the Old Testament is nothing less than a formal introduction to God himself. And so it is with anyone seeking a relationship with him. Its supreme significance, its inestimable value, its ultimate purpose, is that it enables all of us, each and every

one of us, if we so desire, the opportunity to begin to comprehend the Incomprehensible. For anyone seeking to come to know the Lord their God, the Lord God of Hosts, the Creator of the Universe, the Old Testament is, in a word, indispensable.

References

Dillard, Raymond B. and Longman, Tremper, III (1995), *An Introduction to the Old Testament.* Leicester, England: Apollos.

Evans, Craig A. (2004), "The Old Testament in the New" in McKnight, Scot and Osborne, Grant R. (eds) *The Face of New Testament Study: A Survey of Recent Research.* Grand Rapids, MI: Baker Academic, a division of Baker Publishing Group, 130-48.

Fee, Gordon D. and Stuart, Douglas (2003), *How to Read the Bible for all its Worth.* Grand Rapids, MI: Zondervan.

Greidanus, Sidney (1999), *Preaching Christ from the Old Testament: A Contemporary Hermeneutical Method.* Grand Rapids, MI and Cambridge, UK: William B. Eerdmans Publishing Company.

Hill, Andrew E. and Walton, John H. (1991), *A Survey of the Old Testament.* Grand Rapids, MI: Zondervan.

Houdman, S. Michael (ed.) (2014), *Got Questions: Bible Answers to the Questions People are Really Asking.* Bloomington, IN: Westbow Press, a division of Thomas Nelson and Zondervan.

Knight, Kevin (ed.) (2009), Tertullian's *Adversus Marcionem.* Available at: http://www.newadvent.org/fathers/03124.htm (accessed 30 October 2016).

Köstenberger, Andreas J. and Patterson, Richard D. (2011), *Invitation to Biblical Interpretation: Exploring the Triad of*

History, Literature, and Theology. Grand Rapids, MI: Kregel Publications.

La Sor, William Sanford, Hubbard, David Allan and Bush, Frederic William (1996), *Old Testament Survey: The Message, Form, and Background of the Old Testament.* Grand Rapids, MI and Cambridge, UK: William B. Eerdmans Publishing Company.

McCartney, Dan and Clayton, Charles (2002), *Let the Reader Understand: A Guide to Interpreting and Applying the Bible.* Phillipsburg, New Jersey: P. & R. Publishing.

McQuilkin, Robertson (1992), *Understanding and Applying the Bible.* Chicago: Moody Press.

Metzger, Bruce M. (1989), *The Canon of the New Testament: Its Origin, Development and Significance.* Oxford: Clarendon Press.

Motyer, Stephen (1996), Entry for "The Old Testament in the New Testament" in Elwell, Walter (ed.) *Evangelical Dictionary of Theology.* Available at:
http://www.biblestudytools.com/dictionaries/bakers-evangelical-dictionary/the-old-testament-in-the-new-testament.html (accessed: 30 October 2016).

Noble, Terence P. (ed.) (2010), *Wycliffe's Old Testament.* Available at:
http://www.ibiblio.org/tnoble/download/Wycliffe-OT-Noble.pdf (accessed: 30 October 2016).

Osborne, Grant R. (1991), *The Hermeneutical Spiral: A Comprehensive Introduction to Biblical Interpretation.* Downers Grove, Illinois: InterVarsity Press.

Pate, C. Marvin, Duvall, J. Scott, Hays, J. Daniel, Richards, E. Randolph, Tucker, W. Dennis Jr. and Vang, Preben (2004), *The Story of Israel: A Biblical Theology.* Downers Grove, Illinois: InterVarsity Press and Leicester, England: Apollos.

Walton, John H. (1994), *Chronological and Background Charts of the Old Testament.* Grand Rapids, MI: Zondervan.

CHAPTER 3

The World of the New Testament

MATTHEW WONG

Introduction

Since the backdrop to Scripture can be unfamiliar to contemporary readers, it is important to reconstruct the New Testament world in order to understand the setting in which Jesus and His early followers lived. Reconstructing the life setting of the New Testament not only equips us to better understand the authorial intent of the New Testament writers, but also enables us to 'stand in the shoes' of first century believers. This is important as biblical faith is not rooted in abstract musings or philosophical ideas, but in the saving actions of the historical Person Jesus Christ (John 1:1-18) who lived and ministered in Roman-occupied Judea and Samaria[1] two thousand years ago. As the Scriptures are couched in a very real cultural and historical context, it is every believer's responsibility to get to grips with the New Testament's background. In this chapter, five key components will be examined that together paint a picture of what life was like in the New Testament world at the time of Christ: [1] History/Politics [2] Economics [3] Religion/Philosophy [4] Society/Culture [5] Environment.

---

[1] The term 'Judea and Samaria' is used throughout this chapter to denote the ancient northern (Samaria [with Galilee to the north]) and southern (Judea) regions of Israel. It is not to be confused with contemporary Israeli uses of the term, which equate Judea and Samaria with the West Bank (excluding East Jerusalem).

History/Politics

Following the Babylonian invasion and exile in 586 BC, the Medo-Persian king Cyrus the Great issued a decree allowing the Jews to return to their homeland where they later set to work rebuilding the Temple and the city walls (Ezra and Nehemiah) (Metzger 2012, 22). From 334 BC onwards, Alexander the Great defeated the forces of Persia and overthrew Darius III. As part of Alexander's conquest, he entered Jerusalem before going on to found Alexandria in 331 BC (Metzger 2012, 22). However, in the summer of 323 BC, Alexander was struck down by fever, leaving his vast kingdom to be divided amongst his seven generals (Metzger 2012, 22). Judea and Samaria first fell under the control of the Ptolemaic Kingdom, ruled by Ptolemy I Soter, before becoming part of the Seleucid Empire, ruled by Seleucus I Nicator (Hatina 2013, 475). Under the Seleucid reign of Antiochus III and later Antiochus IV, Judea and Samaria became widely Hellenised, much to the Jews' displeasure. Jewish opposition to Jason the high priest's attempt to make Jerusalem a Greek city was misinterpreted as insurrection by Antiochus IV ('Epiphanes' or "manifest god") (Metzger 2012, 23) who sacked Jerusalem in 167 BC, massacred any who resisted, and defiled the Temple's altar by sacrificing a swine on it (replacing Temple worship with the cult of Zeus Olympios) (Hatina 2013, 475-76). It is little wonder therefore that the Jews referred to Antiochus IV as 'Antiochus Epimanes' – 'Antiochus the insane' (Metzger 2012, 23).

The process of Hellenisation, that is the spread and influence of Greek culture (including language) over peoples and lands, was passively resisted by the Hasideans ('the pious'), before the Maccabees embarked on a programme of armed opposition (Metzger 2012, 23-4). Initially headed up by Mattathias the priest, they ensured that the Temple was purified, restored to its original purpose, and rededicated in 164 BC (Metzger 2012, 23-4). Under Mattathias' third son Judas Maccabeus ('the Hammerer'), the resistance group succeeded in establishing an independent state in 142 BC. Known as the Hasmonean Dynasty, this period lasted approximately eighty years until 63 BC (Metzger 2012, 25). The Dynasty ended when Judea became a Roman client state in 63 BC and was given a client-king in Herod the Great (ruled 37-4 BC). Though Herod did not officially have jurisdiction over religious affairs (Hatina 2013, 478), he nonetheless exploited his political clout to appoint and depose a quick succession of high priests from insignificant families, thereby weakening Jewish opposition to his rule (Goodman 1997, 255). Herod is perhaps best known for his cruel edict issued at the time of Christ's birth (Matt 2:16),[2] his expansion of the Jerusalem Temple (completed AD 63) and other large building projects such as the city of Caesarea Maritima, and the fortresses of Masada and Herodium (Goodman 1997, 255).

In 4 BC whilst Augustus was Caesar (Luke 2:1), Herod the Great died, creating a dangerous political vacuum and much unrest. This instability was short-lived however, as Herod's kingdom was divided up amongst his three sons: Archelaus, Antipas and Philip. Archelaus was appointed ruler over Judea and Samaria; Antipas was given Galilee and Perea (south Transjordan), whilst Philip the tetrarch received the territory north-east of the Sea of Galilee (Luke 3:1) (Bruce 1998, 197). Archelaus had a fearsome reputation amongst the Jews (Matt 2:22) and was known to purposefully offend Jewish religious sensitivities – incestuously marrying a Cappadocian princess and appointing/deposing high priests according to political whim (Bruce 1998, 198). He was banished by Augustus to Vienne in Gaul for fear that his rule would spark a full-scale Jewish revolt (Bruce 1998, 198).

Judea and Samaria was governed by a Roman official (or prefect) appointed by the Emperor (Bruce 1998, 199), of

---

[2] When Jesus began His ministry as a man of thirty, Tiberius Caesar (ruled 14-37 AD) was reigning. Paul's missionary journeys took place under the reigns of Claudius (AD 41-54 – Acts 11:28) and Nero (AD 54-68 – Acts 25:21) (Hemer 1973, 572).

which Pontius Pilate is the most well-known. Just like Archelaus before him, Pilate gained satisfaction in offending the Jews, sparking a near-revolt by bringing military standards bearing the Emperor's image into Jerusalem (Bruce 1998, 201). On another occasion he affixed golden shields devoted to pagan deities inscribed with the Emperor's name to the wall of Herod's palace in Jerusalem, though they were eventually taken down on the Emperor's orders (Bruce 1998, 201). He also used the Temple treasury to fund the construction of a new aqueduct – money the Jews believed to be wholly devoted to God (Bruce 1998, 201).

Antipas features prominently in the Gospels (Mark 8:15; Luke 13:31; 23:6-12) and is known for having John the Baptist executed on account of the prophet's willingness to confront the ruler's incestuous relationship with Herodias (Mark 6:17-29). His mix of deviousness and ruthlessness led to Jesus denouncing him as a "fox" (Luke 13:32). He built Tiberius as a tribute to the Emperor, and rebuilt Sepphoris in Galilee (Bruce 1998, 203). In sharp contrast to Archelaus and Antipas, Philip was a mild ruler who only occasionally left his territory (Bruce 1998, 202). He is known for rebuilding Panion as his capital and naming it Caesarea Philippi (not to be confused with Caesarea Maritima built by his father) (Bruce 1998, 202). Eventually, Herod the Great's grandson Agrippa I (ruled 41-44 AD) inherited Antipas' domain (Galilee), and in AD 41 became ruler over the entire region his grandfather once controlled (Hatina 2013, 483). Agrippa I had James the Apostle killed and Peter imprisoned (Acts 12:1-3) before he was struck down by God (Acts 12:20-23). He was succeeded by Herod Agrippa II (Acts 25:13, 23-27) (Bruce 1998, 210).

With such a vast empire, Rome needed to keep control of its provinces to guard against revolt and uprisings. The type of provincial governor installed in various city states was determined by the size, prestige and wealth of the state. For example, proconsuls were installed in Cyprus and Corinth (Acts 13:7; 18:12), prefects in Thessalonica (Acts 17:6), asiarchs in Ephesus (Acts

19:31) and magistrates in Philippi (Acts 16:22, 35, 38). Additionally when required, military presence could be established anywhere in the empire prone to revolution or insubordination. Each Roman province fell into either Senatorial governance (comprising ex-consuls and ex-praetors) or Imperial governance; provinces in the latter category were more volatile or prestigious and directly controlled by the Emperor himself (Metzger 2012, 36). Rome was quick to put down any rebellion, and the Zealot revolt from AD 66 was met with brutal force that culminated in the sacking of Jerusalem in AD. 70.

Economy
As the lifeblood of the Roman economy, trade was greatly facilitated by a vast road network that incorporated major cities and numerous ports allowing soldiers, grain, goods and commodities to be easily transported in and out of Judea and Samaria (Oakley 1962, 12). The free movement of people meant that sellers and buyers were able to travel far afield in order to reach new customers or purchase exotic goods. Lydia, for example, a dealer in purple cloth, travelled hundreds of miles from her home in Thyatira to sell her produce in Philippi (Acts 16:14) (Oakley 1962, 11). Within Judea and Samaria itself, produce and commodities such as fruit, grain, olive oil, wine and bread would have been traded regionally. Trade was not limited to agrarian consumables though, as archaeological finds in the Galilee area suggest the existence of regional trade in clay, pottery, basalt and millstones (Downs 2013, 162).

The most common jobs in first century Judea and Samaria were agricultural based, and many found work on landed estates where wealthy landowners paid workers a daily rate to tend the vineyards, harvest the grain, and look after livestock. The continual purchasing of land by the wealthy elite who imposed taxes on owners and tenants alike meant that most could not afford to own or tenant land themselves. Other jobs undertaken included carpentry (producing stools, threshing sleds and furniture), leatherwork (tanning, which was often located outside the village due to the smell), textiles (dyeing cloth, spinning and weaving), fishing, pottery, stonemasonry (limestone and marble), metalworking, grain harvesting, and grape and oil pressing (Dowley 1999, 24-5). The wealthy and educated could find employment as lawyers, public orators and politicians.

The Romans imposed taxation on independent lands and industries via the ruling classes, and tribute fed directly back to the Empire. They deliberately left economically poor areas unconquered (Goodman 1997, 100) and worked with the Herodians – the Jewish establishment of their day – to ensure that the Imperial tribute, as well as land and animal taxes, were imposed on the people. Different forms of Roman taxation existed, such as *tributum soli* which was a land-based plot-size-dependent tax, *tributum capitis* which was a poll tax based on the size of a workforce, *phoros* which was tribute collected by 'publicani' (senate officials) on an ad-hoc basis (Downs 2013, 163), and *portoria* which was a tax imposed at ports, frontiers and provincial boundaries (Goodman 1997, 100). According to Josephus, the motive behind Quirinius' unpopular census in Luke 2:2 was the registration of property so that accurate land taxation could be calculated and enforced (Josephus, 18.3). Via heavy taxation, Rome ensured the economic and social suppression of its provinces.

Whilst there is some debate regarding the extent of Herodian taxation on Judea and Samaria, ranging from moderate to unbearable, it must be remembered that the Jews were also obligated to pay religious 'first' and 'second' tithes in addition to a yearly half-shekel Temple tax (Bruce, 1972 39). According to one scholar therefore, "the level of combined taxation – civil and religious – for first century Jews may have been around 30-40%, or even higher still" (Grant 1926, 105). Intolerable levels of Roman taxation were likely contributory factors that led to the birth of the Zealot movement.

Religion & Philosophy
The religious and philosophical backdrop to the New Testament is highly complex, with Judaism and

Christianity representing two distinct voices amidst an array of philosophies, gods and Roman mystery religions. The two Greek philosophical schools mentioned in Scripture are Epicureanism and Stoicism (Acts 17:18-21, 32), both of which denied the reality of an afterlife/immortality of the soul. The former affirmed a materialist belief that the senses are the sole criterion of all truth, and taught that wisdom is achieved by living in a state of detachment from external influences (Metzger 2012, 75). Stoicism was a reaction to the irreligious and hedonistic tendencies of Epicureanism. It sought to create a moral rationale for dignified and virtuous living by teaching the importance of living in accordance with universal reason/Logos, demonstrated by the world's natural order and beauty (Metzger 2012, 75-6). Central to its belief was the idea that the soul contained a divine spark or seed of universal reason/Logos, which though only a spark, was proof that one could transcend negative external influences by adopting an unaffected 'stoical' demeanour (Metzger 2012, 76). Though not directly mentioned in Scripture, a number of other Greek philosophies existed in the New Testament world, such as Platonism, Aristotelianism, Pythagoreanism, Cynicism, Skepticism, and Eclecticism.[3]

At the time of the New Testament, people were turning away from classical mythology (i.e. the pantheon of gods) due to the rise of rationalism, the questionable morality of some of the characters in Homer and Ovid's works, and a renewed longing for personal, heart-felt communication with a deity (Oakley 1962, 15). This disillusionment gave rise to a fusion between Greek and Roman polytheism, the latter often characterised by the veneration of local deities (Acts 14:12-13; 19:26-27) (France 1973, 498). This religious hybridisation saw Greek deities renamed as Roman ones; for example Artemis (Acts 19:24-27) was known as Diana, whilst Zeus and Hermes (Acts

---

[3] For more information on these philosophical schools, see Metzger 2012, 74-8.

43

14:11-13) were known as Jupiter and Mercury (France 1973, 498). Greco-Roman religion also included astrology, magic, mystery religions, Gnosticism and divination, mostly originating from the East. Many of the mystery religions involved a process of initiation, with baptism, ritual enactments, costume dressing, communal meals, blood sacrifice, frenzied dancing, intoxication, and debauched activity common (Metzger 2012, 79-86). Avoiding pagan associations in general was a particular challenge for first century Christians; especially as trade guild meetings and banquets were commonly held in pagan temples that served meat offered to idols (1 Cor 8; 10:14-30). Christians who refused to partake in such events often risked being ostracised and losing valuable trade and income as a result.

It was against this religious background that the Jews continued to worship Yahweh. A protected religion, Judaism comprised a number of sects, namely the Scribes, Sadducees, Pharisees, Essenes and Zealots. The Scribes were expert interpreters of the Torah (Matt 13:52; 23:1-3; Luke 11:46) akin to biblical exegetes of today. The Sadducees were a wealthy elite who rejected belief in the supernatural (resurrection, spirits and angels, immortality of the soul) (Matt 22:23-33; Luke 20:27; Acts 23:8) and refused to accept any revelation beyond the Pentateuch. They appear as opponents of Jesus and His followers and collude with the high priest to have the apostles arrested (Acts 4:1-22; 5:17-18) (Lee-Barnewall 2013, 222). The Pharisees, on the other hand, affirmed belief in the supernatural (immortality of the soul, future judgement of believers, resurrection, angels and demons). Unlike the Sadducees who accepted only the written Torah as authoritative, the Pharisees believed that both the written Torah *and* Oral Law (a body of laws and interpretations believed to have been transmitted by God to Moses on Mt. Sinai) were authoritative. In the New Testament they are mentioned in a mostly negative light (cf. Luke 13:31) due to their 'holier than thou' attitude, religious hypocrisy, and willingness to place people under bondage to legalism

(Matt 3:7; 16:6, 11-12; 23:1-39; Mark 3:6; John 11:47-57) (Metzger 2012, 51).

The Essenes were what many scholars believe to have been an ascetic, apocalyptically-focused group based in various towns in and around Judea, but favouring the Dead Sea/Qumran area. They diligently studied the Scriptures, strictly observed the Torah, isolated themselves from Jewish society, and lived as part of a tight-knit community by sharing all things in common (Barnewall 2013, 224; Bruce 1972, 84; Metzger 2012, 52-3). Their religious exercises involved ritual ablutions, baptisms, extended prayer times, and the wearing of white robes to symbolise purity (Metzger 2012, 52-3). The Zealots, though politically-oriented in desiring to overthrow the shackles of Roman oppression, were also driven by a religious zeal that resented any ruler exercising authority over the Jewish nation except God Himself. By engaging in armed opposition to Roman rule, their revolutionary antics sparked a series of revolts that eventually culminated in the destruction of Jerusalem in AD 70. Into this melee of Jewish sects might be added the Samaritans who, after having intermarried with the Assyrians following the invasion of Samaria in 722 BC, were regarded by most Jews as a 'mongrel race'. They famously opposed the rebuilding of the city walls during Ezra and Nehemiah's time, and constructed their own Samaritan temple on Mt. Gerizim overlooking Shechem (John 4:20) (France 1973, 497).

Evidently, the New Testament world was searching to find meaning and purpose in a confusing array of religions, cults and philosophies. The Jews eagerly awaited a political Messiah and failed to recognise the Lord in their midst. To the Greeks and Romans who esteemed worldly knowledge above all else, the idea that God would send His Son to die on a cross – a Roman form of execution reserved for insurrectionists and criminals – was "folly" (1 Cor 1:18). But to those early disciples of Jesus who had heard Him teach, believed His message, and witnessed His miracles, the Gospel was the power of God for salvation.

As Christianity grew however, it began to part ways with Judaism. Consequently, "the Way" (Acts 9:2; 19:9, 23; 22:4; 24:14, 22) – which had hitherto been regarded as *religio licita* under the protected status of Judaism – became the object of intense persecution by Roman Emperors.

Social/Cultural

Thanks to the lingua franca of Latin, people from diverse regions could trade, socialise and live together as fellow citizens in a Roman Empire. The church leadership at Antioch is a fine example of a cross-cultural and multi-ethnic assembly of people who had all found a living faith in the Person of Christ (Acts 13:1). Judea and Samaria was also a thriving cosmopolitan region, alive with trade and industry. Few Jews could speak Latin well, and most conversed in Greek (especially in the area "Galilee of the Gentiles": Isa 9:1; Matt 4:15), Aramaic (the mother tongue for many) and classical Hebrew (spoken mostly by rabbis and scribes) (Metzger 2012, 39). In contrast to contemporary Western society's emphasis on material gain and self-progression, first century Mediterranean culture was collectivist and prized group-belonging and stability; emphasising group honour and 'the collective good' over personal social advancement.

At the top of society were a minority elite who held economic resources, estates, wealth, privilege and power. Beneath them were the senatorial and equestrian classes who had either acquired or inherited their position. Beneath them were the slave class – the largest social group – followed by the peasant classes and finally, at the bottom of society, the underclass. Peasants comprised the people of the land (the *am ha-aretz*), whilst the underclass attracted the likes of outlaws, thieves, mercenaries (Matt 20:1-16), prostitutes and beggars. It is interesting to note that slaves were not considered the lowest in society for they retained some stability in terms of 'employment'. Peasants, however, were often required to hire out their labour on a daily basis and could not be guaranteed regular work.

Slaves were commonplace in the first century Roman Empire, comprising approximately sixteen to twenty percent of the entire population, or a higher percentage still if the total number includes those who had at some point in their lives been slaves (Bartchy 2013, 170). The children of slaves automatically became slaves at birth and it was not unusual for parents to sell their children into slavery for financial reasons, or in some cases, in the hope of improving the child's future (Bartchy 2013, 171). Beatings, torture and execution of slaves – sometimes by crucifixion or burning – were not uncommon (Bartchy 2013, 171) and slaves would sometimes escape their master's clutches by running away (Phlm 12) – a risky decision that was punishable by death.

There is, however, evidence to suggest that the spread of Stoicism gradually led to more civilised attitudes towards slaves in the Empire (Oakley 1962, 14). Greek slaves in Rome were often better educated than their earthly masters and were sometimes entrusted with important responsibilities. An educated slave who served his master well was a valuable possession and could even be loved as a family member (Bartchy 2013, 173). Slaves could purchase manumission (freedom) via a peculium – personal savings accrued during a period of service – and a large number of slaves could expect to be freed by the age of thirty (Acts 6:9) (Bartchy 2013, 173-74), unless the slave chose to remain in his master's service. Whilst the New Testament neither condemns nor condones slavery, the radical message that in Christ "...there is neither slave nor free" (Gal 3:28), that both believing slaves and earthly masters have a Heavenly Master (Col 4:1), and mutual commands for slaves/masters to honour/respect each other (Eph 6:5-9) certainly challenged the prevailing social order of the time.

Entertainment in New Testament times was varied and included chariot racing, gladiatorial combat, athletics, drama, declaration (oratory) and music (Jackson 1969, 16-23). At the time of Herod the Great, there were annual contests held in honour of Augustus, a theatre and amphitheatre in Jerusalem, gladiatorial battles in Jericho, a circus in Caesarea, a hippodrome in Terichaea, and a stadium in Tiberius where one thousand, two hundred Jews would eventually be killed by Vespasian (Jackson 1969, 20, 24). The Jews tended to regard these forms of entertainment as pagan and resented the blasphemous presence in Jerusalem of buildings devoted to carnal, bloodthirsty and sensual pleasure (Jackson 1969, 24). Many were repulsed and horrified by the gratuitous loss of human life in the arenas and consequently steered well clear of such events (Jackson 1969, 24). The less bloodthirsty spectacle of Greek athletics often drew vast crowds and it is interesting to observe the Apostle Paul's use of figurative language associated with athletics to illustrate the believer's duty to press on in the faith (1 Cor 9:24-27; Phil 3:13-14; 2 Tim 4:7) (Jackson 1969, 25).

It goes without saying that life was particularly difficult in New Testament times. With notoriously short life expectancies from birth, the spectre of death loomed large for many. The New Testament world was one blighted by violence and bloodshed, disease and poverty, the practising of magic arts, and fear of demonic influences (Bolt 1998, 77). It was a world imprisoned by an unremitting fear of death's inevitability and its bleak irreversibility. Into this world stepped the Lord Jesus Christ who established the kingdom of God (Mark 1:15) and offered freedom and blessed release to all "those who through fear of death were subject to lifelong slavery" (Heb 2:15) (Bolt 1998, 77). Paul repeatedly re-affirms the truth that death is not the end for Christians, but is rather the means by which Christians receive their final, eternal reward (e.g. 1 Cor 15:55; 2 Cor 5:8; Phil 1:23). Christ's triumph over death therefore enabled New Testament believers, even in the face of death, to find hope in Christ's coming kingdom, and needless to say remains an inexhaustible source of strength and comfort for believers experiencing testing and trials today.

Environment

At the time of the New Testament, many Jews were still living in the Dispersion after having been exiled following the Babylonian captivity in 586 BC. There, outside the Land, Jews continued to observe the Torah and retained their ethnic and religious identity. Diasporic Jewish life became an increasingly attractive option under Alexander the Great who conquered and unified vast territories, "from Macedonia to Babylon and back around to Egypt" (DeSilva 2013, 273). The centres with the largest Jewish populations in the first century AD were Egypt, Alexandria, Syria Antioch and Babylon, though Jewish communities could be found across the Mediterranean as people went in search of family and a better standard of life (DeSilva 2013, 272-73). We can see something of the extent of the Dispersion by the list of lands that the Jewish worshippers had come from on the day of Pentecost in Acts 2:5-11.

Judea and Samaria is central to the Gospel narratives as the birthplace of Christianity in the Ancient Near East. It had a total population of around one-and-a-half to two million, of which just over half a million were Jews – the majority of whom lived in the southern region of Judea (Metzger 2012, 48). Though contemporary uses of the term 'Palestine' are often embroiled in politically charged debate, the name derives from the Hebrew 'peleshet' (translated "Philistia") and appears in Exod 15:14; Ps 60:8, 83:7, 87:4, 108:9; Isa 14:29, 31 and Joel 3:4 to refer to a strip of land on the south-west coast of Israel occupied by the Philistines. In 132 AD, Emperor Hadrian built a Roman colony on the site of Jerusalem and renamed the city *Aelia Capitolina* – a key decision that precipitated the Bar-Kochba revolt of 132-135 AD. After the Romans crushed the revolt, Hadrian in 135 AD renamed the entire province of Judaea – which incorporated Judea, Samaria and Idumea – 'Syria Palestina'. By renaming the Jewish homeland as a perpetual reminder of Israel's historic enemies – the Philistines – Hadrian's insulting appellation has stuck to this day. Not only does the term carry innate anti-Jewish prejudice; it has unfortunately been frequently misappropriated by contemporary politico-religious groups to support their own political anti-Jewish agendas.

The extent of the Roman Empire during New Testament times was vast. The area surrounded the Mediterranean Sea and was bound by the Atlantic to the west, the Euphrates to the east, the Rhine and Danube to the north, and desert to the south (Oakley 1962, 6). In contrast, Judea and Samaria was a small region that lay nestled between the continents of Europe, Asia and Africa, making it the ideal place for the Gospel of salvation to spread throughout the world (Metzger 2012, 21). The region has various climatic zones, from Mediterranean coastal climates, to cold, hot and semi-arid areas; and in terms of topography boasts mountains, deserts, coasts and plains. Though there are marked regional climatic variations, the preponderance of a Mediterranean climate and an abundance of fertile soil meant that Judea and Samaria produced a vast array of fruits as well as sustaining diverse flora and fauna. This diversity and abundance also extended to natural resources; the region being rich in salt, sulphur, bitumen, phosphorous and tar, with particular abundance around the Dead Sea region.

The mix of good soil, rainy winters and hot summers meant that Judea and Samaria produced vast quantities of grapes, olives, and different types of grain. Olives grew in abundance and were a prominent staple of the Judean diet. They were pressed to produce oil, which was used in cooking and as fuel for lamps (Matt 25:3-4), as well as being processed to make soap and ointments for wounds (Dowley 1999, 19). Grapes were eaten fresh, dried as raisins, or pressed for their juice, which could then be fermented as wine (Dowley 1999, 19). The main grains produced were wheat, barley and millet, and though barley was not as popular as wheat, it could be grown on less productive soil (Dowley 1999, 16). Once the soil was softened after the former rains in autumn, it was ploughed and sowed with seed by hand (Luke 8:5-8). After the spring time rains, weeding occurred around December-

February. Harvest time was around April or May when the farmer would thresh the grain (separating the chaff from the grain), winnow it using a large agricultural fork, and sieve it to remove any impurities (Dowley 1999, 16-17).

In New Testament times, Tiberius – built by Herod Antipas in honour of the Emperor – was a major fishing centre and there was a large fish market in Galilee where the day's catch would be presented for sale. Fishing features prominently in the Gospels: Simon and Andrew, as well as James and John were fishermen and many of Jesus' teachings occur around the Sea of Galilee. A number of His miracles either involve fishing or are based in the immediate vicinity of the Sea of Galilee, and He often uses fishing as a vehicle to teach the disciples about the Kingdom of God (Mark 1:17). The main methods of fishing during New Testament times were cast fishing (Mark 1:16) and seine fishing (Luke 5:4), the latter involved the use of a weighted net affixed with corks on the top edge to provide buoyancy. After a hard day's fishing, the nets would have to be inspected and any tears or holes mended. Fishing, particularly on the Sea of Galilee, could be a dangerous pursuit as the mixing of warm and cool air produced squalls that could catch even seasoned fishermen off-guard (Mark 4:35-41 and parallels).

Conclusion
This brief chapter could only ever be a faint sketch of the New Testament world, yet it is astonishing to see how the world was providentially prepared for the arrival of the Gospel in the Person of Christ (Gal 4:4). The geographical location of Judea and Samaria – the 'centre of the world' – enabled the Gospel to spread far and wide, whilst Rome's *modus operandi* provided the infrastructure, common language and movement of people to facilitate Christianity's growth. Moreover, Christ came at a time when many were turning away from classical pantheistic religions and rationalist philosophies. The Gospel provided a new message of forgiveness for sins through Christ's atoning sacrifice, assurance of an afterlife, and

promised followers an intimate relationship with the living God.

However, as important as seeking to understand the world of the New Testament is, it can never be the sole quest for the believer. This is because Scripture, though culture-specific and historically rooted, transcends culture and time. The Gospel, regardless of one's background or place in world history, continues to be the Good News and is as relevant today as it was almost two thousand years ago. We therefore have to learn *how* to apply God's Word to our everyday lives – lives which this chapter has shown are culturally, politically, religiously and in many other ways far removed from the world of the New Testament. How we go about this task, a process known as hermeneutics, is the topic of a subsequent chapter in this book.

References

Bartchy, S.S. (2013), "Slaves and Slavery in the Roman World" in Green, J.B. and McDonald, L.M., eds., *The World of the New Testament: Cultural, Social, and Historical Contexts*. Grand Rapids, MI: Baker Academic.

Bolt, P. G. (1998), "Life, Death, and the Afterlife in the Greco-Roman World", in Longenecker, R.N., ed., *Life in the Face of Death: The Resurrection Message of the New Testament*. Wm. B. Eerdmans.

Bruce, F.F. (1998), *Israel & the Nations*. Rev. edn. Downers Grove, IL: IVP Academic.

Bruce, F.F. (1972), *New Testament History*. Anchor: Doubleday.

DeSilva, D.A. (2013), "Jews in the Diaspora", in Green, J.B. and McDonald, L.M., eds., *The World of the New Testament: Cultural, Social, and Historical Contexts*. Grand Rapids, MI: Baker Academic.

Dowley, T. (1999), *Life in Bible Times*. Oxford: Lion Hudson, Candle Books.

Downs, D. J. (2013), "Economics, Taxes, and Tithes" in Green, J.B. and McDonald, L.M., eds., *The World of the New Testament: Cultural, Social, and Historical Contexts.* Grand Rapids, MI: Baker Academic.

France, R.T. (1973), "The Religious Background of the New Testament", in Alexander, P., ed., *The Lion Handbook to the Bible.* Rev. edn. Oxford: Lion Publishing.

Goodman, M. (1997), *The Roman World 44 BC – AD 180.* Routledge.

Grant, F.C. (1926), "Economic Background of the Gospels" in Bruce, F.F. (1972) *New Testament History.* New York, Anchor: Doubleday.

Hatina, T.R. (2013), "Palestine", in Green, J.B. and McDonald, L.M. (eds) *The World of the New Testament: Cultural, Social, and Historical Contexts.* Grand Rapids, MI: Baker Academic.

Hemer, C.J. (1973), "The Historical and Political Background of the New Testament", in Alexander, P. (ed) *The Lion Handbook to the Bible.* Rev. edn. Oxford: Lion Publishing.

Jackson, D.R. (1969), "Education and Entertainment: Some Aspects of Life in New Testament Times" in *Vox Evangelica,* (6) 4-30.

Josephus, F. *Antiquities of the Jews,* 18.1-4. In Downs, D. J. (2013), "Economics, Taxes, and Tithes", in Green, J.B. and McDonald, L.M. (eds) *The World of the New Testament: Cultural, Social, and Historical Contexts.* Grand Rapids, MI: Baker Academic.

Lee-Barnewall, M. (2013), "Pharisees, Sadducees, and Essenes", in Green, J.B. and McDonald, L.M. (eds) *The World of the New Testament: Cultural, Social, and Historical Contexts.* Grand Rapids, MI: Baker Academic.

Metzger, B.M. (2012), *The New Testament: Its Background Growth and Content.* 3rd edn. New York: Abingdon Press.

Oakley, H.C. (1962) "The Greek and Roman Background of the New Testament" in *Vox Evangelica*, (1) 7-23.

CHAPTER 4

Biblical Exegesis

WALTER LAMBERTI

The meaning and nature of Exegesis

"And now the end has come. So listen to my piece of advice: exegesis, exegesis, and yet more exegesis!" - so declared Karl Barth in his farewell lecture to his students before being expelled from Germany in 1935. But what is exegesis and why do so many Bible scholars, in agreement with Barth, believe it to be so essential? The term is derived from the Greek word ἐξήγησις (exegesis) and means "to be drawn out". In fact, whenever we read any text and seek to understand it we are engaging in exegesis - we are "drawing out" its meaning.

As this definition would suggest, and opposed to some contemporary movements in academia, we regard meaning as present in the text before we as interpreters arrive at the text. That is to say, we do not subjectively assign meaning to a text but instead regard it as a legitimate conduit and repository of meaning. The meaning we seek is commonly referred to as authorial intention. Indeed we instinctively approach texts of all kinds in this way, understanding that something is being conveyed by its author.

Thus, whether we know it or not, all of us are exegetes in our daily lives as we make sense of, and seek to understand, the various writings with which we come into contact. Literature written in our own language and representing our own cultural paradigms require little effort on our part to understand; so much so that we are scarcely aware that we are "drawing out" the author's meaning. However as the distance between the text and ourselves grows, either in time, language or culture, the task becomes more challenging. When we come to the Bible we are confronted with a text (divine inspiration notwithstanding) that predates us by millennia, representing a culture far different from our own and written in languages that are no longer spoken. There is a great need for careful exegesis in order to understand this text from which we are separated chronologically, culturally and linguistically.

It is no accident then that this pursuit of authorial intention is closely associated with grammatical-historical interpretation. As its name suggests, it is an interpretation the focus of which is on both language and history where both contexts are essential in determining an author's original meaning. If we want to know what the author meant in a particular verse we need to know both the textual or literary context of the verse and the cultural-historical context in which the verse was written.

Exegetes pursuing a grammatical-historical interpretation of the text are often said to be pursuing a literal interpretation. At this point we need to qualify what we mean when using the term "literal". A literal interpretation is a not a crude letterism whereby the interpreter is enslaved to the surface structure of the text, but an interpretation that is fully aware of the complexity of written language in its various nuances including symbolism, figures of speech and genre. An interpretation that understands as literal that which an author intended as figurative is no less erroneous than the converse. As God's chosen mode of communication, human language, with all its complexities must be given due consideration.

As such the Bible is not a compendium of timeless aphorisms (i.e. a terse saying expressing a general truth) but a collection of books written over a protracted period of time by different authors in different historical contexts with different purposes and objectives to different recipients. It is resolutely and singularly divine yet variegated and multifaceted in its humanity.

Exegesis in the greater theological task

The larger theological task may be summarised as the move from understanding to application. Application, however, requires that we understand what the text *means* for us today. A question - along with what a text *has meant* (historical Theology) - that can only be answered once we understand what the text *meant*.

This is a distinction that has been championed by E.D. Hirsch (1967) and embraced by a number of bible scholars. Hirsch distinguished between "meaning" and "significance" noting that while the meaning of a text cannot change, its significance can. In other words a portion of scripture cannot mean today what it never meant then. What does change, then, is its significance or application.

Determining what the text meant in its original context is the domain of both exegesis and Biblical Theology. While both disciplines pursue an inductive examination of the text by allowing the text to set the agenda, Biblical Theology focuses on the synthesis of the conclusions derived during exegesis. Exegesis thus provides the building blocks for Biblical Theology. For example, a Biblical Theology of the Pauline corpus is a synthesis of the exegesis of all of Paul's books, which in turn constitutes part of the synthesis of a New Testament Biblical Theology and so forth. In practice there is a reciprocal relationship between the two, and while Exegesis remains the logical first step in the larger theological task, Biblical Theology often informs exegesis just as much as the latter informs the former. This is due, in large part to the fact that meaning is to an extent dependant on context and a Biblical Theology, however formulated, is necessarily a wider context of those portions of scripture of which it is comprised.

Systematic Theology, unlike the first two components does not derive its structure directly from the text of scripture but tends to structure itself topically or logically. Biblical Theology is descriptive and inductive whereas Systematic Theology is prescriptive and deductive (Carson 2000). Systematic Theology focuses on what the text *means* now and formulates the meaning of scripture in ways that address contemporary issues in modern idiom.

As "wide-lensed" disciplines both systematic Theology and Biblical Theology must contend with the unity of scripture within its diversity. For those with a high view of scripture a single Author stands behind the rich diversity of its expression which means that caution must be exercised to avoid, on the one hand, the subjection of this diversity to shallow harmonisation and on the other, the assumption that such diversity is indicative of contradiction.

The final phase and the culmination of the larger theological task whether formulated within a Systematic Theology, a topical study or sermon preparation is, of course, application.

There is much in contemporary society and culture that scripture does not directly address (e.g. genetic engineering and contraception) which means that in order to arrive at some sort of scriptural viewpoint on these and various other contemporary issues much work needs to be done in first understanding scripture in its original context so that applications may be extrapolated for today. This process, borrowing from missiological studies, is often referred to as contextualisation. As Blomberg puts it, "The process of contextualization re-expresses the ideas presented in a biblical passage in the language of today so that they convey the same impact to modern readers" (Blomberg and Klein 2004, 174).

A good example is 1 Cor 11:2-16 in which Paul admonishes the Corinthian women to wear head coverings during prayer or prophesying. How should Paul's directives here be applied today? Was it an issue uniquely applicable only within its first century Corinthian context? Or is it trans-cultural and applicable in any cultural context? In order to contextualise this portion of scripture and extrapolate an application for today we first need to carefully examine its original context.

For example Kenneth T. Wilson has argued, after examining its original context, that the essence of Paul's directives concerning head-coverings was to maintain the male-female distinction (Wilson 1991). He states, "...to require women today to wear head coverings in church is to ask them to do something abnormal rather than normal. This is exactly what Paul wanted to avoid. He wanted women to do what was normal in their culture in reflecting their womanhood and the creative order and distinction" So according to Wilson, in this cultural milieu a woman with uncovered hair had a meaning it no longer does today. How then is it to be applied?

He concludes, "In a broader sense Paul can be understood as asking for appropriate dress in the church—dress that reflects God's intent in the headship of Christ over man and the headship of men over women" (460). Wilson has contextualised what he believes to be the principle undergirding Paul's directives and concluded that for a 21ˢᵗ century western context, a female wearing the appropriate attire in church is sufficient.

It is essential then that we determine how culturally conditioned principles may be applied today. For example, Paul's directives concerning eating food sacrificed to idols would, of course, no longer be applicable in our 21st century context in exactly the same way but the underlying principle of Christian freedom on morally neutral issues whilst ensuring that we do not cause our sibling in Christ to stumble is still undeniably applicable.

While it may be tempting to forgo the challenging task of first determining what relevant scriptures meant in their original contexts before simply pressing them into service of our current needs, it is however precisely this process that ensures our faithful application of that scripture for today. By neglecting this important task we short-circuit the hermeneutical process and run the risk of misapplication – of either "over-applying" or "under-applying" any particular portion of scripture.

The Process of Exegesis

We now turn our attention to the process of exegesis. As we have already sindicated the exegetical process is helpfully summarised by what has come to be known as grammatical-historical interpretation. We shall deal in turn with both aspects of this hyphenated description.

Grammatical Context (*grammatical*-historical)

Here, we are using the term "grammatical" broadly, to denote that which pertains generally to the text of scripture. Literary context may be depicted as concentric circles beginning with a verse's immediate context and increasing to its broadest context, in this case the entire Bible. Between these two are contexts pertaining to paragraphs, individual books, corpora and testaments. There is a rich interplay between all these contexts and much has been written concerning each of them, which extends beyond the scope of this chapter. Unlike most treatments on exegesis we will examine word studies last and present the steps roughly in the order in which they should appear.

1.1 Establishing the Text

First step is textual criticism. Textual criticism is beyond the scope of this paper and thus shall be outlined here in brief. If we are to derive the original meaning of any author the first step is to ensure that the text we have is what they actually wrote. Indeed if the integrity of any text is sufficiently compromised the possibility of arriving at the original authors meaning is slim indeed. Many believers are surprised to learn that we do not possess the original texts (commonly referred to as the "autographs") of either the Old Testament or the New. While such news may be jarring at first, when considering the ancient context of textual transmission the issue is by no means insurmountable. In fact thanks largely to the discoveries of important fragments and manuscripts the critical texts of scripture we now have are more accurate than those of just a few decades ago (Komoszewski, Wallace 2006).

1.2 Determining the Genre

Many books on exegesis place the determination of genre as the first step in the exegetical process. There is good reason for this. The genre of a text effectively determines the rules by which that text should be interpreted. For example, poetry would be interpreted very differently from a legal document. Indeed this step is of such importance that the following chapter will focus on its role in exegesis. Here we shall simply note in passing that it is of critical importance to first determine the genre of a text before arriving at any exegetical conclusions.

1.3 Exegetical Outlining

This involves constructing an exegetical outline of the entire book in question. It may seem unnecessary and cumbersome to construct an outline of an entire book to simply determine the meaning of a particular passage but it is essential to know where within the course of the author's argument the passage in question occurs. For example there is currently much debate surrounding the nature of Paul's argument in Romans 2. Is Paul here viewing the Jews as a subset of fallen humanity or is his critique more pointed and aimed at ethnocentrism? In that case certain passages within Romans 2 take on different meanings. Several outlines exist for each book of the bible and as most will differ at certain places it is worth examining a few.

Discourse Analysis. Discourse Analysis is a relatively new discipline and focuses on the text above the sentence level and deals with aspects such as boundaries, prominence and cohesion within a text or discourse (Runge 2010, 3-15). Among its tenets is the emphasis on the way an argument or discourse develops by giving special attention to the way propositions are connected. This type of analysis is particularly useful as it highlights information typically not even discernible when analysing the grammar and syntax of a passage (see below). Consider Rom 1:15-17 with semantic tags included:

A Thus, for my part, I am eager to preach the gospel to you also who are in Rome.

> B <u>For</u> I am not ashamed of the gospel, REASON
>> C <u>For</u> it is the power of God for salvation to everyone who believes, REASON
>>> D to the Jew first and also to the Greek. CLARIFICATION
>> E <u>For</u> in it *the* righteousness of God is revealed from faith to faith.... REASON

Indentation is used to depict subordination. Note that though the theological freight is within lines B to E, semantically these lines are subordinate to line A. Line B merely gives a reason as to why Paul is eager to preach the gospel also in Rome while Line C and E (which are of equal semantic weight) give reasons for line B. Line D is further subordinate to line C and provides clarification on the phrase "all who believe". It is important when undertaking such an analysis to pay careful attention to conjunctions that indicate transitions in the flow of thought.

It is preferable, particularly from this level and as we progress to smaller linguistic units, to work in the original languages as nuances are often lost in translation. For example, in many instances several words are required in the receptor language to capture an idea in the original. However for those exegetes not trained in Koine Greek with the help of good commentaries, exegetical aids and patience much ground can be covered.

1.4 Grammar and syntax

Next we should seek to trace the argument at the sentence level paying careful attention to grammatical functions of words and the role each plays in the sentence (again, preferably but not necessarily in the original languages).

Not a few exegetical decisions turn on a question of grammar. For example in 1 Corinthians 13:8 the Greek word παύσονται ("will cease") in reference to the gift of tongues occurs in the middle tense. In the debate between cessationists and continuationists a number of the former have argued that the middle tense – as is often the case in koine Greek - implies that the subject acts upon itself. Thus, it is argued, tongues will cease of themselves as opposed to prophecies and knowledge. A number of scholars have pointed out the weaknesses of such an argument but this specific argument nevertheless turns on an issue of grammar (Wallace 1997). There is much to be gained from the study of Hebrew and Greek grammar. For example in Greek there is much to learn simply concerning its use of the article ("the"). Its verbal system and use of participles is particularly fruitful exegetical terrain.

For this reason a number of scholars recommend sentence diagramming, a practice that forces the exegete to grapple with each word in the sentence. In sentence diagramming each element of a sentence is depicted graphically according to its function so that at a glance one can view how the sentence is constructed. Consider 1 Cor 2:10 depicted in a sentence diagram:

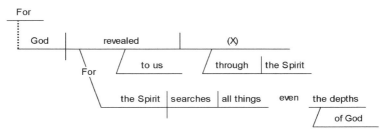

Note however that, as opposed to semantic diagramming above, sentence diagramming will often ignore semantic information especially pertaining to the relationship between verses. Both forms of diagramming have their place as they illuminate different and often complementary aspects of the text (Guthrie and Duvall 1998).

1.5 Lexicology

One of the most exciting and certainly the most popular steps in exegesis is word studies. Indeed for many this constitutes almost the entire exegetical process. It is not uncommon to still find exegetes that seek to simply define each word in the sentence and then conclude that the exegetical task is complete. One need only consider a metaphor to realise that such atomistic exegesis is rarely accurate and should be avoided.

Word studies also happen to be particularly susceptible to errors and exegetical fallacies only some of which we can briefly touch on here (see Carson 1996). The following principles are a good starting point and worth bearing in mind when undertaking word studies.

Firstly, *the form of a word does not determine its meaning.* This is easily demonstrated if we consider the English word "butterfly". The meaning of this word can obviously not be determined by breaking it into its constituent parts, that is, "butter" and "fly". The same applies to our study of Biblical languages. For example in 1 Cor 4:1 Paul states "men ought to regard us as servants of Christ". The Greek word used for "servants" is υπηρετας which is derived from the verb ερεσσω meaning "to row". The basic meaning of υπηρετας then was thought by many scholars to be "rower". The word υπηρετας can be further divided into its constituent parts namely υπο meaning "under" and ερετης meaning "rower". Thus it was concluded by some that when Paul spoke of υπηρετας he had the concept of "under-rower" in mind. Most scholars now recognise this interpretation to be erroneous and based on faulty linguistic assumptions (Louw 1982). It is usage that determines meaning not lexical form.

Secondly, *words have a range of meanings*. Words have a semantic range and the meaning to be "activated" at any point in time is that meaning which is suggested by the context. We should thus avoid the temptation of importing all of a word's meanings into any one context, an exegetical error commonly labelled "illegitimate totality transfer". For example, in Paul's frequent use of the word "flesh" one must be careful to not import all its meanings into every usage but rather let the context determine its meaning in each instance. Sometimes it refers to the weakness of human flesh at other times to our sinful natures. The meaning that most suitably fits the context is likely the meaning the author had in mind.

Thirdly, *word meanings change over time*. For New Testament exegesis the study of classical Greek word usage is of little value precisely because by the time we reach the first century Greek had undergone not a few significant changes. Let us consider an English example. The root of the word "awful" is "awe" but it would be incorrect to assume that in contemporary usage "awful", a word with a decidedly negative connotation, has anything to do with "awe". What is needed is a *synchronic* word study as opposed to a *diachronic* one. The former focuses on usage during the relevant period in question while the latter traces the word's usage throughout its development. While diachronic word studies are helpful and often interesting, synchronic word studies, focused as they are on usage during the relevant period of study, are of utmost importance (Silva 1995).

It must be cautioned that word studies, as important as they are, comprise but one aspect of the exegetical process and cannot be relied upon to settle every exegetical decision. This is partly because, as is increasingly being realised thanks particularly to insights from linguistic studies, words derive their meaning primarily from their context. Thus even biblical language lexicons will frequently give what is referred to as a *semantic range* for a word – the meanings the word can possibly have given its context – so that even then exegetes are required to seriously contend with the context before selecting the appropriate meaning.

Lastly, *we must avoid the tendency of confusing word and concept.* For example if we were to do a study of the concept of "grace" in the New Testament we would need to include more portions of scripture than just those in which the word "grace" occurs. This is because the concept of grace may be expressed in a variety of ways including with words other than "grace" though which may still denote the same concept.

Hermeneutical Spiral

Though we distinguish between the various phases of exegesis, in practice all the phases are intertwined. One cannot understand the whole without understanding its constituent parts; while on the other hand, the whole provides meaning to the parts. An exegete, thus, does not proceed systematically from one step to the next but instead moves back and forth between them at all times during the exegetical process.

Historical Context (grammatical-*historical*)

The second pillar of grammatical-historical exegesis requires careful examination of the culture-historical context in which the text was written. Of course the most immediate context is that which pertains to the authorship, recipients and occasion of each book, information all of which is immensely useful in understanding the argument of the book and, for the most part, readily available. On a larger scale, and somewhat more difficult to grapple with, are the shared cultural assumptions that pervade the pages of each book often appearing subtly through the slightest of allusions.

It must be remembered that Christianity is a historical religion in that God has spoken in time and space, and His words and deeds are couched in human cultures at specific points in time. An accurate understanding of His words therefore requires an understanding of the cultural milieu in which His words were first conveyed. Once again if we are to apply scripture to our lives today we need to first understand what it meant then in that *Sitz im Leben* (a German term common in biblical studies meaning "setting in life").

Firstly, we need to understand that the cultural-historical context of scripture is very different from our own. As Hayes and Holladay note, "as students interpreting biblical materials we are, in a sense, third-party intruders and suffer from third-party perspectives" (Hayes and Holladay 2007, 15). A cursory reading of the Old Testament will reflect vastly different social settings to our own. The historical cultural setting of the New Testament is no less unfamiliar to us at first. It represents a multifaceted intersection of Jewish and Graeco-Roman culture. For example there is much said about issues such as meat sacrificed to idols and circumcision; topics representing overtly Jewish concerns. However it must be remembered that all of this occurred under the aegis of the Roman Empire and steeped in Greco-Roman cultural customs such as patronage and benefaction (Green and Macdonald 2013).

Not only does it require effort to investigate cultural-historical settings but the issue is further complicated by our own natural propensity to read and interpret through our own cultural paradigms. While the idea of approaching the text as a *tabula rasa* (blank slate) is commendable, in practice it is not possible. This is because all exegetes are reading from "somewhere". We as humans are always culturally conditioned and inevitably read within the framework of our own cultural paradigms and worldview.

However, we are not hereby doomed to a subjective interpretation of scripture. What is required is the awareness, as far as possible, of our own assumptions – a process often referred to as "distantiation". Only then can we hope to "spiral" (once again) into the text's true meaning. As Carson puts it,

> Whenever we try to understand the thought of a text . . ., if we are to understand it critically . . . we must first of all grasp the nature and degree of the differences that separate our understanding from the understanding of the text. Only then can we profitably fuse our horizon of understanding with the horizon of understanding of the text-that is, only then can we begin to shape our thoughts by the thoughts of the text, so that we truly understand them. Failure to go through the distantiation before the fusion usually means there has been no real fusion: the interpreter thinks he knows what the text means, but all too often he or she has simply imposed his own thoughts onto the text (Carson 1996, 26).

Armed with the awareness of our own assumptions we may proceed to examine the cultural-historical context of the text. Indeed there are certain historical questions that we are currently not in a position to answer (and perhaps never will). For example in 1 Cor 15:29 we read, "Otherwise, what do people mean by being baptised on behalf of the dead? If the dead are not raised at all, why are people baptised on their behalf?" While many suggestions have been put forward as to the identity and meaning of those baptised for the dead, we cannot say with any level of confidence to whom Paul was referring.

Nevertheless, there is much we do know and many historical questions we can answer thanks to the wealth of tools that are now available on almost all aspects of

Biblical historical context, ranging from Bible dictionaries and commentaries to specialised monographs and archaeological studies.

Conclusion

It has been said that exegesis is both science and art. The former because the process involves many definable steps and the use of appropriate tools; the latter because the precise methods we use and tools we deploy depend on the passage in question. Indeed twenty-first century believers are in the unique and privileged position of having more and better exegetical tools than any generation that has gone before, but what is still needed is the discernment of which tools to use and when to use them. Indeed for some passages of scripture the exegetical questions turn solely on issues of grammar, for others a single word may change the tenor of the entire paragraph, for still others the primary issues are historical. Such discernment is only developed by constant use, but as it develops the process takes on the form of art.

However, whether science or art, what is needed, as always, are interpreters who take seriously the interpretation of the scriptures as God's word and are willing to spend time and effort in the glorious task of uncovering its meaning. As we indicated above, this is never the end of the larger theological task, but instead, the necessary starting point for its application in our lives and contemporary contexts. If we understand what its Author was saying then we can know what He is saying to us today. In this case we echo Barth's sentiments: "exegesis, exegesis and yet more exegesis".

References

Carson, D.A. (2000), "Systematic Theology and Biblical Theology" (pp 89-104) in *New Dictionary of Biblical*

Theology: Exploring the Unity & Diversity of Scripture. Edited By Desmond T. Alexander and Brian S. Rosner (IVP Reference Collection) Leicester: Inter-Varsity.

Carson D.A. (1996), *Exegetical Fallacies.* Grand Rapids, MI: Baker Academic.

Green, Joel B., and Macdonald, Lee M. (2013), *The World of the New Testament: Cultural, Social, and Historical Contexts.* Grand Rapids, MI: Baker Academic.

Guthrie, George H., Duvall J. Scott (1998), *Biblical Greek Exegesis: A Graded Approach to Learning Intermediate and Advanced Greek.* Grand Rapids, MI: Zondervan.

Hirsch, E.D. (1967), *Validity in Interpretation.* Yale University Press.

Klein, William W., and Blomberg, Craig L. (2004), *Introduction to Biblical Interpretation.* Thomas Nelson.

Komoszewski, Ed J., and Wallace, Daniel B. (2006), *Reinventing Jesus.* Kregel Publications.

Louw, J.P. (1982), *Semantics of New Testament Greek* (Society of Biblical Literature Semaia Series). Society of Biblical Literature.

Runge, Steven (2010), *Discourse Grammar of the Greek New Testament: A Practical Introduction for Teaching and Exegesis.* Hendrickson Publishers.

Silva, Moises (1995), *Biblical Words and Their Meaning.* Grand Rapids, MI: Zondervan.

Wallace, Daniel B. (1997), *Greek Grammar Beyond the Basics: An Exegetical Syntax of the New Testament with Scripture, Subject, and Greek Word Indexes.* Grand Rapids, MI: Zondervan.

Wilson, Kenneth T. "Should Women Wear Headcoverings?" in *Bibliotheca Sacra* 148:592.

CHAPTER 5

Genre and Biblical Interpretation

ANTHONY ROYLE

Introduction

Interpreting the Bible can be difficult when approached from a twenty-first century Western perspective. The Scriptures were written by various authors who lived over two thousand of years ago, from within a different culture and in three different languages. Today's readers are therefore separated on many levels from the world of the Bible and this causes many difficulties. Certain expressions that the authors intended to convey to the original readers may be misunderstood, which has sometimes led interpreters to read as allegorical a passage that may have been meant as literal, or interpret something literal that was meant to be symbolic.

As many Christians simply pick up their Bible and begin to read a few verses or chapters, taking the words at face value, the original meaning can easily be missed and replaced by the reader's own assumptions and worldview. Gordon Fee and Douglas Stuart argue "the only reason we must not begin with the here and now is that the only proper control for hermeneutics is to be found in the original intent of the biblical text". (1993, 25) If the reader's interpretations are not guided by the original meaning of the text, then the text can mean whatever the interpreter desires. Fee and Stuart warn that "a text cannot mean what it never meant". (Ibid, 26). Therefore, it is important for the interpreter of the Bible to read the Scriptures through the eyes of the author and original readers. But is this possible? And if so, how does a twenty-first century reader accomplish this?

One important approach seeking a solution to this interpretive problem is a focus on literary forms (or genre), in other words, styles of literature. The Bible exhibits various styles of literature—or genres—for example, history, poetry, legal writings, songs, and so on. Biblical scholar Tremper Longman III notes the work of Hermann Gunkel (1862-1932) who proposed that literary forms developed out of life settings and traditions within communities. (1985, 49) This means that by recognising a piece of literature's genre, the reader can determine the authorial intention behind the passage, the culture of the original audience, and their worldview.

Various scholars have noted, for numerous reasons, the importance of identifying a book's genre within the process of Biblical interpretation, while others have suggested that the notion of genre is a concept originating with Greek philosophers such as Plato and Aristotle, and therefore, has no meaning to the original Jewish authors (Osborne, 2006, 181). However, it appears the biblical authors did not write in a literary vacuum and wrote within the style of related literature. Therefore, determining the genre of a specific text and applying the relevant rules on how to interpret that genre will assist the biblical interpreter in bridging the gulf between when the ancient texts were written and those reading them today.

This chapter focuses on biblical genres and consists of two sections. The first lists and explores five reasons why genre is important to Biblical interpretation and the discovery of the meaning of the text. Building upon this, the second section surveys the various genres of the Bible and their characteristics.

The Importance of Genre in Biblical Interpretation
There are five reasons why identifying and understanding genre is important in the task of Biblical interpretation.

1. Understanding genre helps the reader to know whether the author meant something literally or figuratively

Certain genres lend themselves more to figures of speech, metaphors, allegories, and hyperbole. For example, poetry and parables indicate that the author is communicating in a figurative manner. Likewise, apocalyptic writings also employ symbolic images and should often be interpreted in a similar manner, while on other occasions those symbolic images require a literal interpretation. Epistles also contain some figures of speech, which are a little harder to discern given that generally the epistles are to be taken literally. The particular rules of the genre of epistles, however, do help the reader understand when the author is writing figuratively. The historical narratives and law material are intended to be read literally. Historical narratives are intended to record the historical events of God's people. Laws within legal codes are intended literally as guidelines and commands for people to follow. Also, many of the legal codes fit a pattern or a type that is used symbolically, but that does not negate the fact that the reader should interpret the text literally.

The reader can know when a piece of literature is poetic because of its structure and its use of metaphors. Alternatively, historical literature testifies of historical people and describes historical events in the form of narrative, which are read and understood literally. The reader should not interpret poetry in the same way as interpreting historical narrative because those metaphors and symbols would be taken too literally. Likewise, to interpret historical narrative in a similar manner to poetry would indicate the events recorded as merely proverbial. So, categorising a piece of literature is important in order to avoid misreading what is written.

It is sometimes difficult to recognise whether some books are poetic or historical. The early chapters of Genesis are often considered to be historical narrative and poetry by others. The genre classification of Genesis clearly impacts upon whether or not the interpreter attributes a literal meaning to the seven days of creation, Adam and Eve, and the Fall. So it is imperative to accurately identify the genre as a precursor to establishing the correct meaning in Scripture.

2. Genre expresses the thoughts and beliefs of a particular culture in a certain period of history

Literary kinds are formed from within cultures and social settings. Groups of writings that form a category tend to come from a particular period in a culture's history. Gunkel in particular considered the Psalms to have emerged from a period of David's life and therefore present an idea of David's cultural setting (Gunkel, 1967, 36-39). The apocalyptic writings, both canonical and apocryphal were written during similar periods in Jewish history presenting similar but also contrasting worldviews. The legal codes from Exodus through Deuteronomy reflect the period in which the Law was written, and can be compared with the legal codes of Ancient Near Eastern nations. Likewise, the epistles reflect the apostolic era and give insight into the world and life of the early church, while also reflecting conventional Greco-Roman writing traits, via, for example, Paul's use of the introductory formulae "from A to B, greetings", as well as preserving Semitic phrases such as "grace and peace to you" (Stowers, 1986, 21).

3. Genre highlights the importance of contemporary writings

As genre expresses a certain culture and its worldviews during a particular time, contemporary writings to the Biblical books, of the same genre, are also important. Longman writes "The grouping of texts in genres is a necessary prerequisite to comparative studies". (Longman 1985, 66) One of the most important collections of contemporary literature to the New Testament was the sectarian writings known as the Dead Sea Scrolls. This is a collection of writings that were discovered in caves near the Dead Sea (1946-1956), and thought to belong to an exclusive Jewish community at Qumran during the period preceding and contemporary to early Christianity (approximately from 408 BC to 318 AD). These writings included multiple genres but reflect an interpretation of the Jewish Scriptures that is similar to the interpretations of the New Testament authors. Some of these writings contain instructions on how the group should live, and are similar to instructions found in the words of Jesus and also in the epistles. This highlights some of the similar or even competing views of this same period of time in Israel. Also, some of the writings in the Dead Sea Scrolls are eschatological and predict future events through interpretations of the Hebrew prophets in similar ways to the Gospels and epistles. This provides insight to some of the eschatological expectations of the day and that both the Qumran community and early Christians viewed their own movements as fulfilling Scripture.

4. Genre helps the reader understand the form and structure of the text

A piece of literature will generally contain a form or structure with rules of a particular genre (Ibid, 51). For example, a narrative will be structured with a beginning, a sequence of events that provoke the protagonist(s) to action, which resolves itself with a conclusion. When interpreting the narrative, the reader should establish what happened at the beginning of the story and then understand where the story is leading. Knowing the genre places the words within a context.

Likewise, poetry is written with certain patterns and structures. When the reader identifies these structures it helps the reader to understand what the author is communicating through the composition of the text. In Proverbs in particular, there is a distinct pattern of two line sayings. The first line is the *mashal*, a proverbial statement, while he second line is a *nimshal*, an interpretive statement that clarifies the meaning of the *mashal*. For example, Proverbs 1:17-18:

> 17 For in vain is a net spread
>   in the sight of any bird,
> 18 but these men lie in wait for their own blood;
>   they set an ambush for their own lives.

The first stanza in verse 17 is the *mashal,* using an analogy of a net before bird in order to catch it as a pointless and self-defeating exercise. The second stanza in verse 18 is the *nimshal,* which explains that those who lie and wait to do wicked things to others ironically are causing harm to themselves.

2.5 Genre helps the reader know what questions to ask of a text

Identifying and understanding genre is the beginning of the interpretative process. Once a genre is established the interpreter must start asking relevant questions about the text. For example, in interpreting an epistle, questions of authorship and recipients are of great interest as the epistle is a communication between the two. The relationship between Paul and some of the churches he wrote to provides insight into what Paul is communicating. Knowing who Paul is and his journeys also assists in establishing the context of an epistle.

In reading the historical narratives, the reader should ask questions regarding the historical context of the period the book was written, a portrait of the historical figures from other sources, what the political situation was like, the geography of the places involved, and many other questions regarding settings and culture.

Genres in the Bible
The Scriptures contain multiple genres, which have been categorised by various scholars. Some disagree with a certain book's genre and some recognise that there are books that contain a mixture of genres. For the sake of this

study I want to focus on eight genres that are recognised by the majority of scholars.

Old Testament	New Testament
Law	Gospel
Historical Narratives	Parable
Wisdom	Epistle
Prophecy	Apocalyptic*

* Some Old Testament writings also contain portions of apocalyptic material; however, the main genres of these books are prophecy and / or narrative.

1. Law

The first five books of the Bible, often referred to as "The Pentateuch", are considered as the Law. Contained within these books are six hundred and thirteen commands given to the nation of Israel. The book of Genesis contains no Law codes but is still considered as part of the Law. Within these books are also narratives of the patriarchs, the events of the Exodus, and Israel's wandering in the desert for forty years. These five books narrate the special covenantal relationship between God and the nation of Israel. From a Christian perspective, these laws are considered as part of the old covenant that is no longer binding. Commands regarding what someone should eat are regarded as no longer required in the New Covenant. Peter's vision in Acts 10 that all animals are now clean and the edict given by the Council of Jerusalem in Acts 15 impact how Christians interpret the clean and unclean animals in the law. Similarly, Jesus' declaration of being Lord of the Sabbath and the "greater than the Sabbath" theme in Hebrews 4:6-10 has led Christians to not keep the Sabbath (Saturday). Alternatively, some laws are viewed as still binding. These commandments tend to be centred on ethical issues such as the prohibitions against murder, and false witness, or, by contrast, the continued requirement to honour one's mother and father. The division of moral and ceremonial laws has been a view held since Origen (184-253 AD), implying that the moral law is still binding but the ceremonial law no longer applies. However, some Christians do consider commands such as the prohibition of tattoos as still binding today.

Christopher Wright argues that the division between moral and ceremonial laws does not reflect the unity of Scripture and that the dismissal of ceremonial laws is contrary to Paul's words that all Scripture is profitable for doctrine and training in righteousness (2 Timothy 3:15-17) (Wright, 1992, 225). Wright proposes a method that recognises the objective and function of a particular command and allows the reader to preserve the object but change the context (Ibid, 229-231). Take for instance Paul's use of Deuteronomy 25:4 "You shall not muzzle an ox while it is treading out the grain" (ESV) in 1 Corinthians 9:9. Paul asks the question, "Is it for oxen that God is concerned?" Paul is not substituting himself in place of the oxen but has preserved the objective of the command, which is the diligent care in using someone else's property. In this case the context changes from a neighbour's ox working in the fields to God's apostle working in the church (See Verbruggen, 2006, 699-711).

2. Historical Narratives

The Old Testament writings tell the story and history of Israel from before the calling of Abraham to the return to the land from the Babylonian captivity (approximately 538 BC). Some of this story is conveyed in prophetic form but mostly there are substantial portions of the Old Testament that are historical narratives. The Biblical books considered as historical narratives are Joshua, Judges, Ruth, 1 and 2 Samuel, 1 and 2 Kings, 1 and 2 Chronicles, Ezra, Nehemiah, and Esther. Other books contain large portions of historical narratives, such as Genesis, Exodus, Numbers, Deuteronomy, Jonah, and Daniel; however, those books also belong to other genres.

Although historical narratives are recordings of events that happened, they are composed of narratives told in a certain way that has structure and contains literary devices. Plots thicken and characters develop, and often these narratives contain a moral lesson. However, the Scriptures are historically reliable and the reader should be aware of the potential pitfall of decontextualising a passage by stripping away all of its historicity or allegorising a passage beyond the original meaning of the text. The reader does not have to strip the history of the text away to grasp the meaning of the text, but should rather understand the story in the place of history to interpret what the author is trying to communicate. Not every narrative explicitly declares whether the actions of some are good or bad, nor does a narrative give the reader a complete theological picture of what has occurred. Furthermore, narratives do not necessarily indicate what is descried as normative for Christians today. In order to grasp the moral and theological scope of the passage the reader should understand the narratives as part of the bigger picture (meta-narrative).

3. Wisdom

Wisdom literature covers numerous genres. The Wisdom books of the Bible are Job, Psalms, Proverbs, Ecclesiastes, and the Song of Solomon. Each of these books differ in their use of genre, but all may be categorised under the rubric of Wisdom literature. Grant Osborne notes that the unifying characteristics of Wisdom literature of the Scriptures is that they are practically orientated, exhibit or exhort a dependency on God, have indirect authority, and are theologically reflective upon creation (Osborne, 243-246).

Psalms. The Psalms are a genre in their own right as a collection of a hundred and fifty works (not counting non canonical Psalms). The Psalms are poetically composed and must be read individually within the structure of its own Psalm. The reader can recognise the patterns that are present in each Psalm and understand its form, in order to establish the type of Psalm. Some Psalms are lamentations and express the thoughts and feeling of the author that may involve questioning God's justice against the wicked, or God's goodness during tribulation (Psalms 3, 22, 31, 39, 42, 57, 71, 120, 139, and 142). Some Psalms are hymns of thanksgiving and praise and were used by Israel in their worship of God (Psalms 8, 19, 33, 66, 100, 103, 111, 113, 114, 117, 145, 146, 147, and 149). These hymns were thankful for God's provision, his covenant, and for salvation. Some of the Psalms also provide an overview of Salvation History, a theological overview of a biblical historical event like the Exodus (Psalms 78, 105, 106, 135, and 136). The Psalms reflections on these events provide insight into the theological significance of the event.

Proverbs. Proverbs are also genre in their own right. These are a collection of brief sayings and some short allegorised parables. Some of these proverbs are riddles, admonitions, confessions, or beatitudes (Ibid, 247-250). At times they are composed in a double stanza of a *mashal* and *nimshal*. Although a proverb can be read independently, Fee and Stuart argue that proverbs must be read as part of the entire collection (Fee and Stuart, 222-223). When some proverbs are read in isolation they may lean towards some inappropriate behaviours, so require the balance of reading other proverbs so not to wander to extremes. For example, if the reader was to isolate Proverbs 21:17 (He that loves pleasure shall be poor: he that loves wine and oil shall not be rich) from the rest of Proverbs, then one would be inclined to deprive themselves from pleasure to avoid financial problems. However, other Proverbs refer to having joy in this life and that oil and wine are blessings from God (Proverbs 3:10). Proverbs also strongly reflect upon ancient culture and do not guarantee a direct translation to other cultures. They should not be read as a guarantee for promises. The use of language is often figurative and therefore in many cases uses hyperbole or exaggeration.

Ecclesiastes. The book of Ecclesiastes also contains sayings like Proverbs, but is often considered the book of Proverbs' cynical brother. The tone is very different and is more reflective on a life without God. Like the Psalms, Ecclesiastes is working out its philosophical thoughts regarding why the wicked prosper and why good things happen to bad people. Therefore, the conclusion of the book is a summary of what the teacher has concluded from these thoughts. Reading each individual saying in isolation, like Proverbs, can lead to inappropriate application.

Job and Song of Solomon. Job and Song of Solomon are different types of Wisdom literature because they are narratives too. Job is a dialogue between Job and his friends with some interjection from God. It is a theodicy concerning Job's suffering. The book is considered wisdom in that there are some practical points from Job's trial as Job depends on God and even theologically reflects upon creation. The Song of Solomon also contains an exchange of dialogue that tells of the highs and lows of a love story between a man and his bride, which rabbis and early church fathers have argued is an allegory for either God's relationship with Israel (R. Akiba) or Christ's relationship to the church (Methodius, 290 AD). Both Job and Solomon should be read with the same cautions of reading other wisdom literature and other narratives. The sayings in these narratives should not be read in isolation and, likewise, the stories should not be allegorised.

4. Prophecy
There are sixteen books that are known as Prophetic books; four Major Prophets (Isaiah, Jeremiah, Ezekiel, and Daniel) and a further twelve Minor Prophets (Hosea-Malachi). These books record some portion of the lives of the prophets; therefore they contain some historical narrative and some apocalyptic visions, but mainly prophecies in which the Lord speaks. The prophets mediated the message from the Lord for their own time. Fee and Stuart name them "covenant enforcers" as the prophets gave messages from God rebuking Israel often because they had

forsaken their covenant with God (Ibid, 167). Additionally, the prophets also spoke of future events. From a Christian perspective, the prophets spoke of Christ, both his first and second coming. However, sometimes a prophecy will be interpreted in a way that was never originally intended. First, the historical context of the prophecy must be established (Ibid, 173-175). Knowing the times, for example, when Isaiah and Jeremiah prophesied helps the interpreter understand the situation into which the prophet, or rather God through them, were speaking. Secondly, the interpreter must establish a prophecy by identifying the oracle (Osborne, 2006, 271). In some of the prophetic writings it is difficult to know where the prophecy begins and where it ends. Osborne uses the examples of the Servant Songs in Isaiah 42-53, which flows through a series of oracles that do not necessarily start and end at the beginning of each chapter (Ibid, 271). Once an oracle has been established then the reader can view the oracle in the context of its surrounding prophecies. (Ibid, 271-272) In the case of the Servant Songs of Isaiah they must be individually interpreted as prophecy, but also belong together to form a singular message within Isaiah.

Subgenres (a genre working subordinately within another genre) are also important in determining the meaning of an oracle. Some prophecies are in the form of poetry or even a proverb. The symbolic nature of prophecies must also be determined. Once the historical and grammatical boundaries are established it is only then that the interpreter asks whether a text holds any Christological or eschatological significance (Ibid, 273). Some passages are direct in their message and others are more analogical (typological), but neither approach contradicts the historical grammatical meaning of the text.

5. Gospel
The genre of the Gospels has been debated by various scholars who have proposed they belong to Jewish historiographies, or even as Midrash. Scholars today prefer to keep the genre of the Gospels distinctly different to

previously proposed genres, although some similarities are evident and even helpful in identifying.

The Gospels are biographical, mainly recording the time of Jesus' ministry unto His crucifixion and resurrection. They contain historical narratives and therefore the historical context of Jesus's life and ministry. Consequently, the time and culture in which He lived are important to understand. Understanding the narrative also helps the reader appreciate the structure of the book. For example, Matthew is structured around five discourses of Jesus, which reflect the five discourses of Moses in Deuteronomy. Matthew certainly wants to draw comparisons between Jesus and Moses. Many of the stories of Jesus reflect similar stories in the Old Testament and the Gospels also have a prophecy-fulfilment pattern with regards to events in Jesus' life, which have led some scholars to argue that the Gospels are a mixture of historical events with some embellishment. Of course each of the Gospels are creatively written by their authors, as they differ in style and language; however, the fourfold set of Gospels are historically reliable. Some of the differences between the Gospels can be viewed as differences in perspective of authors, or stylistic choices. The Gospels are also thought to have originated orally within the early church for the first thirty years therefore, understanding cultures that pass on traditions orally helps the reader understand how the Gospel writings developed.

6. Parable

Parables are longer versions of proverbs. In fact the Hebrew for parable and proverb are the same (*mashal*). Parables are found in the Old Testament as well as in the teachings of Jesus (Isaiah 5, Ezekiel 21 and 24). However, it is in the teachings of Jesus that the genre of parables is mostly focussed. Jesus used examples from everyday life in order to communicate what the Kingdom of God was like, therefore, the parables contain symbolism. However, scholars are quick to note that parables are not allegories. The difference is that allegories give significance to every detail. Fee and Stuart give the example that if one used allegory in the Parable of the Two Debtors (Luke 7:40-42) one would find significance and meaning in the five hundred denarii and fifty denarii (Fee and Stuart, 140). However, parables are to be interpreted according to a singular point, which in this example, is that the one whose debt was great and was cancelled was the most grateful. On this occasion, Jesus offers an interpretive *nimshal*, which helps the reader, but it is the context of the parable that reinforces the singular point being made. Jesus was speaking to a Pharisee named Simon who was scoffing at Jesus allowing a woman who was a known sinner to wash and perfume his feet.

Some parables are given in clusters and can be used to interpret one another. For example, in Luke 15 the parables of the lost sheep, the lost coin, and the prodigal son provide a compilation of parables about the joy of salvation in finding that which was lost. Parables, like proverbs, are to be read in light of one another as they form a picture of what the Kingdom of heaven is like.

7. Epistles

The language of the epistles are perhaps the most straightforward of the genres of the Bible because of how direct Paul, Peter, and others write in order to communicate with their readers. Instructions like "walk in love, just as Christ loved you" (Ephesians 5:2) are very straightforward to interpret. Theology such as "through one man's sin death reigned, how much more the grace of God through one man Jesus Christ abounded for many" (Romans 5:15) needs little further explanation. However, as the apostle Peter highlights, there are some things in the letters of Paul that are difficult to understand (2 Peter 3:15-16).

Some of the writings in the epistles have also been disputed in meaning, therefore, showing that interpretation of the epistles is not always as straightforward as one would expect. Some of these disagreements are on the moral teaching of the epistles and the first century context. For example, should women wear head coverings in church? (1 Corinthians 11:1-16). Understanding of the historical and cultural context is important in approaching these issues, as well as the context of the situation between author and reader. It is also important to follow the logical development of the author's argument and note how he comes to his conclusions. In the case for head coverings, loose hair was a sign of female liberation for temple prostitution to Diana. A covered head was a cultural sign of submission in this case, as it was to be practiced in the context of prayer and worship. Paul makes his point using Christ being the head of the church. Although, head covering is not something that carries the same connotations today, the church still deals with other equivalents in the area of headship and prayer within the church.

8. Apocalyptic

Apocalyptic comes from the Greek work *apokalypsis*, which means "revelation". The term apocalyptic was given to a type of literature where a protagonist would have a heavenly vision or had ascended into heaven and is revealed mysteries of God. Such messages came with offerings of salvation and warnings of judgement. Usually there is a form of dualism (battle between good and evil) in the story and there is a retelling of history or biblical events.

In the Old Testament there are various sections that are considered apocalyptic. Although Daniel is considered one of the four Major Prophets, much of his visionary experiences recorded in the book are considered apocalyptic (Daniel 7-12). The same with the heavenly experiences in Isaiah 6, Ezekiel 1, and Zechariah 1-6. There are various shades of apocalyptic events such as Jacob's vision (Genesis 28:12), Sodom and Gomorrah (Genesis 19), Joseph's dream (Genesis 37:9). And also some apocalyptic descriptions in the teachings of Jesus (Mark 13) and Paul (Romans 8). Then there is the book of Revelation, a series of heavenly visions recorded by John as a message for his own time and for the return of Christ. There is also a wealth of apocalyptic writings written around the time of the Second Temple period (approximately 530 BC to 70 AD) that also contribute to the understanding of apocalyptic as a genre.

Some find apocalyptic, especially the book of Revelation, difficult to interpret as the genre is rich in symbolism. And in contrast to the poetical and parabolic genres of the bible, apocalyptic has historical reference. The events that are being described are historical events or will be events that happen in the future. Some apocalyptic descriptions are of nations and Empires. Some are of people. It is not always easy to determine who or what these symbols are. Sometimes the Scripture offer an interpretation of a particular symbol. Sometimes common symbolism between apocalyptic writings can be identified. However, the reader should be diligent in making sure that any correspondences between symbol and historical reference completely match.

Conclusion

Each book of the Bible clearly fits into a pattern of structure or style that are identifiable with other pieces of literature of similar kind. The Scriptures were not written in a vacuum in a dictatorial fashion by the Holy Spirit. The Spirit moved the authors of the Bible to express the Word of God using their own vernacular and creativity, which the reader can identify by interpretation through genre analysis. Although there are arguments that genre is a manufactured lens for reading the Bible that was not in the mind of the original authors, it remains that literature of similar kinds offers the reader insight into how to interpret the Scriptures.

It is when the reader deconstructs the Bible away from any historical meaning and disregards any literary context, that the reader begins to have a plethora of vain interpretations regarded as "my own personal interpretation". The reader should not read the Bible in a vacuum, awaiting an exoteric interpretation, but rather be guided by the Spirit in study. When the reader approaches the Scriptures with sensitivity to genre and acknowledges how a certain genre works then one can begin to read the Bible through the eyes of the original readers and begin to grasp and understand what the text means.

Identifying and understanding genre is just the beginning of the process. Once the reader has established the necessary information about a piece of literature's genre that the meticulous process of exegesis begins, moving from the macro-level to the micro-level of interpretation. From there the reader may begin to analyse rhetoric, semantics, grammar and syntax, spiralling towards the meaning of the text.

References

Engle, R. W. (2000), "The Use of Genre in Biblical Interpretation" in *JMAT 04:1*.

Fee, Gordon D. and Stuart, Douglas (1993), *How to Read the Bible for all its Worth* (Grand Rapids, MI: Zondervan.

Gunkel, H. (1967), *The Psalms* (trans. By T. M. Horner). Philadelphia: Fortress Press.

Howe, T. A. (2007), "Does Genre Determine Meaning?" in *CAJ 06:1*.

Longman III, Tremper (1985), "Form Criticism, Recent Developments in Genre Theory, and the Evangelical" in *WTJ 47:1* (Spring).

Osborne, Grant R. "Genre Criticism- Sensus Literalis?" in *TRINJ 04:2* (1983).

Osborne, Grant R. (2006), *The Hermeneutical Spiral.* Downers Grove, IL: IVP.

Stowers, Stanley K. (1986), *Letter Writing in Greco-Roman Antiquity.* Philadelphia: Westminster Press.

Verbruggen, Jan L. (2006), "Of Muzzles and Oxen: Deuteronomy 25:4 and 1 Corinthians 9:9" in *JETS 49:4* (December).

Wright, Christopher J. H. (1992), "The Ethical Authority of the Old Testament: A Survey of Approaches. Part I" in *Tyndale Bulletin 43:1*.

Wright, Christopher J. H. (1992), "The Ethical Authority of the Old Testament: A Survey of Approaches. Part II" in *Tyndale Bulletin 43:2*.

CHAPTER 6

Christian Doctrine

THOMAS FRETWELL

Introduction

The study of Christian theology is the highest activity in which the mind of man can be engaged. To procure for oneself a knowledge of the living God is an activity of immeasurable value and infinite worth. This knowledge will impact every area of a person's life, their understanding of the world around them, how they behave, and even their understanding of reality itself. The great Swiss theologian Karl Barth offers a beautiful description of the pursuit of Christian theology, in which he likens it to gazing upon the great and beautiful landscapes of Tuscany, which hold the viewer in awe on account of the breath-taking views in which they offer. So too, according to Barth, is the view offered by studying Christian theology. To search out and discover the knowledge of God by studying the doctrines of the bible can truly be one of the most exhilarating, challenging, and yet rewarding experiences of life.

It is with this conviction that we shall proceed with the introductory survey of Christian doctrine. This chapter is not designed to overload readers by seeking to make them conversant with the vast sea of theological minutiae that have developed over the past two thousand years, nor is it the intention to burden readers with the necessity of grasping a whole new vocabulary before they can begin to study theology. Instead, this chapter is designed to provide the reader with a basic understanding of what comprises orthodox Christian theology from an Evangelical perspective, and equip them with the tools to go deeper in their quest if they desire to do so. This chapter will therefore give those who work through it a good foundational knowledge of what we mean by theology and doctrine in a Christian context, why it is so important to study doctrine, how to navigate doctrinal disputes, and finally, the practical benefits that manifest in a person's life when doctrine is properly applied.

Preliminaries

Before proceeding we need to establish a working definition for a number of terms. First of all, the basic term "theology" can be construed in a number of ways. In its most basic etymological sense it simply means "thinking about God". Coming from two Greek words, *theos* meaning "God" and *logos* meaning "discourse" or "rational expression". In this sense everyone is a theologian. Whether one considers themselves an amateur or professional does not matter, theology is for everyone. Even the atheist is in some way a theologian, having positively rejected the existence of God, and expressing that rejection in statements or creeds, he falls under the remit of this definition of theology, he is thinking about God – he thinks God does not exist and discourses on why he thinks this.

Yet, it is necessary to provide a richer definition of the term as we use it within a Christian context in order to explain properly what it is a theologian actually does. Theologian Millard Erickson provides a good comprehensive definition in his book *Christian Theology* when he states that theology is

> That discipline which strives to give a coherent statement of the doctrines of the Christian faith, based primarily upon the scriptures, placed in the context of culture in general, worded in a contemporary idiom, and related to the issues of life. (Erickson, 2006, 23)

Erickson further suggests a number of specific ingredients that go into making this definition of theology more understandable: (1) Theology is biblical, meaning content is drawn from its primary source the canonical scriptures, both the Old and New Testaments, utilizing the tools and methodology of biblical research (as well as allowing for insights from General Revelation); (2) Theology is systematic, attempting to avoid using texts in isolation from one another, rather drawing on the entire Bible in order to present a coherent body of teaching; (3) Theology is relevant, in that it interacts with various other disciplines such as cosmology, psychology and philosophy; (4) Theology must be contemporary, meaning that it must relate God's truth to the questions and issues of the time; and (5) Theology must be practical, not simply as creedal declaration of doctrinal truths, but applicable to practical living as well (2006, 23). These ingredients help us to understand in a broad sense the basic concepts conveyed by the use of the term "Christian theology". As previously stated, theology involves explaining the doctrines of the Christian faith. So we now turn our attention to this term "doctrine" and make sure we understand its meaning and usage in theological discourse.

The term doctrine comes from the Greek word *didaskalia* and refers to an act of teaching, or instruction. This term can be used of any sort of teaching or information that is passed on. For example, in the Bible we have the word being used to speak about the teachings of men (Mark 7:7-8), and also the teachings of demons (1 Tim 4:1). Yet the most common usage in the biblical text is to refer to the teachings of God, those beliefs that make up the authoritative content of divine revelation. Christianity is a religion that is based upon certain non-negotiable truths. In Scripture then, we see the term doctrine being applied to the entire range of theological truths that accurately portray the whole message of Christianity. Wayne Grudem gives the following definition: "A doctrine is what the whole Bible teaches us today about some particular topic" (Grudem, 1999, 20). Simply, doctrine is a biblical exposition of theological truths.

A comment regarding the source of these doctrines is necessary. The ultimate source of all Christian doctrine is the triune God who has purposefully and graciously willed to reveal Himself to us (Matt.11:25-27; 1 Cor. 2:10-12; John 1:18). Although God is the ultimate authoritative source of doctrine He has chosen to reveal doctrine to us through His prophets and the apostles as recorded in the Bible. The Bible itself declares that "All Scripture is breathed out by God and profitable for teaching (doctrine), for reproof, for correction, and for training in righteousness" (2 Tim. 3:16). The Bible is the source of sound doctrine for today. Theology conducted from an evangelical confessional standpoint will hold this presupposition: "The Bible is true and that it is, in fact, our only absolute standard of truth" (Grudem, 1999, 21).

One other specific usage that we find in the Bible is worthy of consideration here. Given that the term doctrine refers to the theological truths as outlined in the Scriptures, this leaves open the reality that their negation is also possible; false doctrine, i.e. the corruption of true doctrine, either by misinterpretation or deliberate exploitation. The New Testament contains many exhortations to resist false doctrine. Paul writes to Timothy warning him; "For the time will come when they will not endure sound doctrine; but *wanting* to have their ears tickled, they will accumulate for themselves teachers in accordance to their own desires" (2 Tim. 4:3) (cf. 1 Tim.6:3-4; 1 John 4:1).

Doctrine and the Church
Christianity and doctrine are indispensable to each other; the one cannot exist without the other. True Christianity will be firmly grounded in the doctrines of the Bible. From its earliest days the Christian faith was formulated in doctrinal terms and great emphasis is given to its importance in the Scriptures. The early Christians were exhorted to "pay close attention to yourself and to your teaching (doctrine)" (1 Tim. 4:16). They were encouraged

to be faithful to the apostolic teaching which was "from the beginning" (1 John 1:1-4), and to "contend earnestly for the faith which was once for all handed down to the saints" (Jude 3:3). The message of the apostles was the "standard of sound words" and believers are exhorted to "guard...the treasure which has been entrusted to you" (1 Tim. 1:13-14). Ministers of the Gospel are also exhorted to "entrust these to faithful men who will be able to teach others also" (2 Tim. 2:2) and to be "constantly nourished on the words of the faith and of the sound doctrine which you have been following" (1 Tim. 4:6). The Apostles were committed to ensuring that the authoritative body of teaching they had received was protected and propagated by the early Church in order that the proclamation of the gospel would continue (1 Phil. 1:7).

The apostolic teaching that is found in the New Testament highlights the four main propositions that formed the core of apostolic doctrine and preaching. (1) Jesus was the Christ, the promised Messiah of the Old Testament (OT). This doctrine provided continuity with the already existing body of revelation found in the OT, bridging the gap between the Old and New covenants. Jesus was the fulfilment of many OT prophecies and thus the promised saviour of Israel and the world (cf. Acts 3:18, Luk3 24:27). (2) That Jesus was to be put to death (Acts 2:23). Jesus was crucified on a cross according to the predetermined plan and foreknowledge of God (cf. Acts 5:30, Phil.2:8). (3) That He was risen from the dead. This served as the fulcrum of apostolic testimony, the event to which all could be pointed to provide confirmation of all that Jesus said and did (Acts 2:24). The apostles made much of the fact they were eyewitnesses to these events (Acts 3:15, Luke 24:48). Later in the epistles of Paul we see him systemising the theology of the resurrection as it relates to our justification (Rom. 4:24-25), our reconciliation (Rom. 5:11), our baptism and relationship to sin (Rom. 6:1-5), the indwelling Spirit (Rom. 8:11), our future resurrection (1 Cor. 6:14), and the essential nature of the resurrection to our faith (1 Cor. 15:17). (4) Finally, salvation could only be procured by exercising faith in Jesus name (Acts 3:16, Acts 4:12). These fundamental teachings made up the basic core of apostolic doctrine. Of course, doctrine itself is broader than just these truths, and they were still preached in conjunction with already existing truths of the OT, but they did constitute the bulk of the "body" of sound doctrine that emerged from the early church, which was to be "once and for all delivered unto the saints" (Jude 1:3).

The study of doctrine was fundamental to the ecclesiology of the early church. The book of Acts tells us that the early church "devoted themselves to the apostles teaching" (Acts 2:42). The word for devoted means "exerting great effort to persist in doing something" (Rydelnik, 2014, 1678). It shows us that the study of doctrine is to be a continuous and habitual process in the lives of believers both then and now.

As the New Testament cannon was completed and the first generation of believers began to die out, there was a surge in aberrant doctrine being promoted by people professing apostolic authority. In order to ensure that these aberrant works were unable to circulate and cause confusion among the larger church it became necessary for the early church to formulate written statements of their beliefs. These became known as creeds – from the Latin word *credo*, "I Believe". Alister McGrath states that a creed

> Has come to be recognised as a concise, formal, and universally accepted and authorized statement of the main points of the Christian faith. (McGrath, 2011, 14)

The period of Church history known as the Patristic period (c.AD 100-700) bequeathed to the church three famous creeds: The Apostles' Creed, the Nicene Creed, and the Chalcedonian Creed. These creeds have gained wide acceptance within the body of Christ at large. The Apostles' Creed, written in the third-fourth century, is perhaps the most well-known creed today, even after almost two thousand years. It provides a good summary of early Christian beliefs:

> **The Apostles' Creed**
> I believe in God, the Father almighty; Maker of heaven and earth.
>
> And in Jesus Christ his only Son, our Lord; who was conceived by the Holy Spirit, born of the Virgin Mary; suffered under Pontius Pilate, was crucified, dead and buried[1]; On the third day he rose from the dead; he ascended into heaven; he is seated at the right hand of God the Father Almighty; from thence he will come to judge the living and the dead.
>
> I believe in the Holy Spirit; the holy catholic[2] and apostolic Church; the communion of saints; the forgiveness of sins; the resurrection of the body; and the life everlasting. Amen. (Grudem, 1999, 473)

Over the course of church history, we have seen the development of a number of different methods for studying theology and doctrine. While there is obviously a symbiotic relationship between these methods as they interconnect at various points, they can still be distinguished from one another. The most common being Systematic Theology, this method is easily identifiable by the way it systematically organises the biblical material under different doctrinal headings. For example, a textbook of Systematic Theology will contain the following chapters; Bibliology (the doctrine of the Bible), Soteriology (the doctrine of salvation), Christology (doctrine of Christ) Ecclesiology (doctrine of the church), Eschatology (doctrine of the end times), and so on.

---

[1] The phrase "he descended into hell" is not included as it is not attested in the earliest versions of the creed.

[2] This phrase meant universal, not Roman Catholic as we would assume today.

Systematic theology has proven extremely helpful as a means of providing Christians with a clear and comprehensive way to present the fundamental doctrines of the Christian faith. Systematic theology is to be distinguished from other common methods such as Biblical theology – which incorporates both OT theology and NT theology and has a narrower focus of study usually focusing on a particular author or time period, or on biblical themes, or historical theology – which focuses on what has been taught by theologians and by the pronouncements of Church councils throughout history. All of these methods have been used by theologians to further the study of Christian doctrine.

Why Study Doctrine?
We have seen that in the Bible the exhortations to study doctrine are plentiful. But why? For what purpose does the psalmist say "teach me good discernment and knowledge, for I believe in your commandments" (Psa. 119:66)? Why does the apostle Paul repeatedly pray for those he ministers to that God may give them; "a spirit of wisdom and of revelation in the knowledge of Him" (Eph. 1:17), and why does Peter exhort his readers to "grow in the grace and knowledge of our Lord and Saviour Jesus Christ" (2 Pet. 3:18)? Answering these questions is what the study of theology is all about. Theology is not intended to be a cold pursuit of faceless doctrines listed in black and white on the page before you, rather the pursuit of doctrine is nothing less than the burning desire to see God in full colour, to see into the very throne room of God and understand more of the nature and character of the great God we worship!

For many Christians the word "doctrine" is misunderstood, seen as something that academics concern themselves with in their ivory towers, and so these Christians who have misunderstood the concept offer simple platitudes such as "I don't do doctrine, just give me Jesus", or "it's about deeds not creeds". Arguably, in some cases they do so in order to circumvent the necessity of engaging in the study of Christian doctrine. Tragically, this sort of amorphous faith that seeks to divorce Jesus from the doctrines concerning him is misguided. As we have seen, studying the doctrines – the content of our faith is a clear and unmistakeable command of scripture and absolutely vital to the Christian life.

This is the most fundamental reason for studying doctrine: the Bible simply commands us to. If we are true followers of Christ this should be enough. In order to be part of the Great Commission we must be able to impart doctrinal truths to others. In the great commission Jesus commanded us to "teach" others what he has commanded:

> Go therefore and make disciples of all nations, baptizing them in the name of the Father and of the Son and of the Holy Spirit, teaching them to observe all that I have commanded you; and behold, I am with you always, to the end of the age. (Matt. 28:19-20)

Far from the being the purview of a few gifted evangelists this aspect of the Great Commission is to make disciples by teaching them to observe what Jesus taught, in order to be part of this we need to have a good grasp of biblical doctrine. In an equally famous passage of Scripture, Jesus commands his followers to come and learn from him (Matt. 11:28-30), exhortations to study the scripture abound (cf. Prov.9:9; 2 Tim. 3:14). It is as we study the Scriptures that we learn more of the nature and character of God, his purpose in creating us, his will for us, his love for us, we learn about the doctrine of salvation, about what it meant for Jesus to die on the cross as a substitute for our sins. These precious truths of the Christian faith are all doctrinal affirmations, rooted in real history, and seeking to understand them is how we mature in our Christian faith (Eph.4:13-15; Heb.5:12-13; 1 Pet. 2:2).

Safety and Guidance
Although many may think of doctrine as just the accumulation of facts, a view I hope we have already

shown to be in error, it can still be difficult for many to grasp how doctrine will benefit them practically. It must be understood that there is an essential link between sound doctrine and your spiritual life. The things we believe about God will always influence how we behave in relation to God and those around us. Wrong doctrine often leads to wrong actions and vice-versa. The pattern in the epistles is to outline first the correct doctrinal understanding of various truths and then provide practical instruction on how they should be lived out. The link between the two is indispensable and any disparagement of doctrine in favour of the more emotional aspects of the "spiritual life" such as worship, merely demonstrates a misunderstanding of both concepts. Our emotions must be informed by a correct understanding of God, gained through his revealed truth, and from this our worship will be enriched as we worship God in spirit and truth (John 4:24). Correct doctrine provides a pattern for right living. Paul writes to Timothy that the law is good if one uses it lawfully. He then provides a list of moral activities which he classifies as "contrary to sound doctrine" (1 Tim. 1:9-11). Elsewhere when instructing Titus on the qualifications for elders he lists a number of moral qualities that should be present in leaders, among which is to hold fast the faithful word; "which is in accordance with the teaching, so that he will be able both to exhort in sound doctrine and to refute those who contradict (Titus 1:9).

This raises another vital reason for studying doctrine: it keeps us away from false doctrine which can be harmful to our lives, both physically and spiritually. We know that certain men have crept in who seek to turn the grace of God into a license for immorality and deny the Lord Jesus (Jude 1:4). We know the early Church was having to confront those who were preaching a "different gospel" (Gal. 1:6) and that false teachers would be introducing "destructive heresies" that deny Christ (2 Pet. 2:1). It is only a knowledge of the word of God that can ensure, "we are no longer to be children, tossed here and there by waves and carried about by every wind of doctrine, by the trickery of men, by craftiness in deceitful scheming" (Eph. 4:14). The command to be well versed in biblical doctrine is vital for every Christian who desires to live a godly life in Christ Jesus.

Navigating Doctrinal Disagreements

It is crucial to point out that not all doctrinal disputes fall under the banner of false doctrine. Caution, wisdom, and humility must be exercised in identifying what is false doctrine and what may be merely a denominational disagreement, or a difference that relates to a secondary doctrine. This highlights the need to establish a proper doctrinal taxonomy and a working definition of "major" and "minor" doctrines. Grudem provides the following guideline:

> A major doctrine is one that has a significant impact on our thinking about other doctrines or that has a significant impact on how we live the Christian life. A minor doctrine is one that has very little impact on how we think about other doctrines and very little impact on how we live. (1999, 21)

This definition is helpful, but still allows for a measure of subjectivity, as what one may think impacts other doctrines to a certain degree will vary from person to person. To refine this idea further, we could say that major doctrines are the non-negotiables of the Christian faith, those doctrines which if abandoned would mean that one effectively ceases to believe the Christian Gospel. A minor doctrine would be something that Christians can disagree over due to interpretive differences, but has no effect on their status as a Christian. They can disagree but still retain a large measure of unity with each other because the major doctrines of the faith are held in common. Under this definition some examples of major doctrines would be the doctrine of the Trinity – believing in the Trinitarian nature of God rather than a strict monadic concept such as that held by Islam, or a teaching that redefines the person of

Christ by denying his divinity, or his sinless nature. Another would be justification by faith – any teaching that adds human works to the finished work of Christ, all of these would constitute a repudiation of a major doctrine which would fall into the category of false doctrine as they remove you from orthodoxy into heresy (1 John 4:1-3). Some examples of minor doctrines would be the method of baptism, the correct form of Church government, matters of eschatology, such as the timing of the rapture and the great tribulation. In these cases, Christians may prefer to go to a fellowship or denomination that affirms their belief, but as should be obvious, both still fall within the bounds of historic Christianity as they affirm the major doctrines together and thus can have true fellowship with one another and these differences should not be allowed to cause fleshy division (1 Cor. 1:10).

Evangelical Beliefs
The word Evangelical is derived from the Greek term in the Bible for "gospel", which means good news, referring to the message of Jesus. In this sense anyone who is devoted to sharing the message of Jesus could be classed as an Evangelical. However, although in this sense evangelicalism is not a recent innovation, it has become associated with a specific movement prevalent during the 19th and 20th centuries within Protestant Christianity. The theological roots of Evangelicalism can be traced to the Reformation of the 16th century. The doctrinal core of the Protestant reformation, led by people such as Martin Luther, Ulrich Zwingli and John Calvin, focused upon the rediscovery of foundational doctrinal truths that had been lost under the oversight of the Catholic Church and the Papacy. The Reformation summarised these truths in what have become known as the five *Solas* of the Reformation:

1. *Sola Scriptura* – (scripture alone). The revealed word of God in the Old and New testaments is our final authority and must always take precedence over personal experience or ecclesiastical authority.

2. *Sola Fide* – (faith alone). Justification is by faith alone and no human work can contribute anything to our salvation.

3. *Sola Gracia* – (Grace alone). Salvation is an unmerited gift of God's grace and nothing we do can go towards deserving salvation.

4. *Solus Chritus* (by Christ alone). Salvation is given only by a saving knowledge of his son Jesus Christ.

5. *Soli Deo Gloria* (solely for the glory of God). Everything, including our salvation is accomplished in order to reveal God's glory. (Jones, 2005, 566)

These five Solas are now associated with Reformed theology, sometimes simply referred to as Calvinism. The Reformers themselves differed on the finer points of theology concerning the five solas, but broadly speaking they undergird much of protestant theology today and provided a foundation for the emerging evangelical movement. Evangelicalism's distinctive characteristics were not fully formed until the great Evangelical Awakenings of the eighteenth century. The famed American preacher Jonathan Edwards along with two English clergymen, George Whitfield and John Wesley, preached the principles of justification by faith and the new birth across America and England bringing revival to these nations.

It is from these historical and theological streams that modern Evangelicalism grew. Drawn from this background David Bebbington has listed four central themes that have characterised Evangelical belief ever since. First, evangelicals were Conversionist, that is, they recognised the need for people to receive the gospel. Secondly, they were Activist, meaning they understood the need for energy to be spent propagating the gospel. Thirdly they were Biblicist, the Bible was the final authority. Fourth, they were Crucicentric. They saw the centrality of the cross in the gospel (Bebbington, 1989, 4-8).

Now Go and Do the Same

Having briefly surveyed the doctrinal landscape of Christianity we need to ask an honest question: now what? In Luke's gospel (10:25-37), Jesus responds to a question from a Pharisee regarding the command to love your neighbour. He answers by telling the story of the Good Samaritan, and after telling the parable He asks the Pharisee for the correct interpretation. The Pharisee, answering correctly, identifies the Samaritan as the one who proved to be a true neighbour by showing mercy, demonstrating that he understood the point of the story. Jesus then issues a command to the Pharisee; "Go and do the same." (Luke 10:37) What he is in effect saying is go and live out your faith. The doctrinal teaching of love your neighbour (Lev.19:18) must now be practiced in the lives of those who understand it. The command is the same to us today, go and live your life in accordance with sound doctrine.

The beliefs we have should impact our Christian lives for the glory of God. The Apostle Paul writes to Titus that we are to "be well-pleasing, not argumentative, not pilfering, but showing all good faith so that they will adorn the doctrine of God our Saviour in every respect" (Titus 2:10). The Amplified version is particularly expressive in its rendering of this verse phrasing it in this way: "So that in everything they may be an ornament and do credit to the teaching [which is] from and about God our Saviour" (Amplified Bible). The imagery of an ornament is familiar; for instance, we hang them on Christmas trees to make them attractive. The word for "adorn" is the Greek word *kosmeo* which means to decorate, to put in order, or make beautiful. From this root we get the English word cosmetics, the products women use to make themselves more beautiful. This language provides us with a powerful and beautiful picture of what right doctrine does in the Christian life. The doctrines of

God are what make the Church, the bride of Christ, beautiful. As we exhibit these doctrines through our conduct, we are accurately representing God to the world. We should seek to do this in such a way that people will "see your good works, and glorify your Father who is in heaven" (Mat. 5:16). Elsewhere Paul conveys a similar point writing that Christians are letters of Christ, "known and read by all men" (2 Cor. 3:3). The act of "adorning" our lives with the doctrines of Christ is to be a habitual practice, indicated by the use of the present tense in Titus 2:10. Christians are to continually radiate the beauty of Christ by lives that are consecrated to Him. Such a life requires that the precious doctrines-the great truths of Christianity, are studied, loved, lived and even sung in such a way that glorifies our God in heaven.

> O Word of God incarnate,
> O Wisdom from on high,
> O Truth unchanged, unchanging
> O light of our dark sky,
> We praise Thee for the radiance
> That from the hallowed page,
> A Lantern to our footsteps,
> Shines from age to age.

> (Bishop How - Methodist Hymn Book)

References

Bebbington, David (1989), *Evangelicalism in Modern Britain; A History from the 1730s to the 1980s.* London: Unwin Hyman.

Erickson, Millard J (2006), *Christian Theology* 2nd Ed. Grand Rapids, MI: Baker Academic.

Grudem, Wayne (1999), *Bible Doctrine: Essential Teaching of the Christian Faith.* Leicester: Inter-Varsity Press.

McGrath, Alister E (2011), *Christian Theology: An Introduction*. Chichester: Wiley-Blackwell.

Rydelnik, Michael; Vanlaningham, Michael (2014) eds., *The Moody Bible Commentary*. Chicago: Moody Publishers.

Jones, R.T. "Reformed Theology" in Ferguson, Sinclair; Wright, David, ed., *New Dictionary of Theology*. Leicester: Inter-Varsity Press.

CHAPTER 7

Biblical Prophecy and the End Times

CALVIN L. SMITH

The Bible is not merely a collection of narratives of events, historical records, theological discussions, laws, poetry, commandments, and so on. As a unified and divinely inspired collection of writings, it tells a story. We might call this the Bible's story, or more technically the canonical narrative (that is, the over-arching narrative that runs through the canon of Scripture).

This Bible story begins with God creating the world and the first humans, how those humans sinned, and the subsequent effect upon the rest of humanity. The story continues with God raising up, first, the Patriarchs, and later, the people of Israel, through whom He revealed His salvific plan for all of humanity. Through God's covenant with Israel He gave the law, which demonstrated (among other things) the holiness of God, humanity's inability to be truly holy, and thus the need for a saviour. God also sent the Prophets to provide Israel with news of a future hope. The Bible story continues with God sending a Jewish Messiah - the Saviour foretold by the Prophets - who was crucified and rose again. The story continues with how this Jewish Messiah's sacrifice extends salvation to all humanity, the rise of the Church and the inclusion of the Gentiles, and the spreading of Gospel throughout the known world. Associated with this part of the story is the emergence of challenges and problems, both theological and practical, and how church leaders called by God (notably the Apostle Paul) were used by God to respond and, accordingly, shape the theology, ethics and practices of this new Church.

However, the Bible story does not end with the successful spread of the Church throughout the Roman Empire. This is merely the end of one stage of the Bible story, indeed it is more or less where the events recorded in the Bible end. But that is not to say that when John wrote the Book of Revelation towards the end of the first century, that is the end of the Bible story itself. The Bible has a considerable amount to say about the future, which is the culmination of the canonical narrative. Issues such as how Christ returns, what is happening in the world at the time, how He will deal with the nations, what happens to believers who have died since Bible days, and what happens in eternity, are all discussed in the Bible and together comprise the culmination of the Bible story. This is precisely why eschatology (the study of the last times) is – or should be – so important for Christians.

Thus, having briefly outlined above how the end times represent an integral aspect of the Bible's story, this chapter aims to provide readers with an introduction and brief survey to the topic as a starting point for further study. It is divided into three parts. The first explores the concept of the kingdom of God as set out in Scripture, how this theme serves as an important rationale for the centrality of eschatology in Christian thought, and why it ought to shape all believers' great eschatological hope. This is followed by a brief examination of the different ways Christians have sought to systematise the Bible's teachings on the end times and categorise eschatology, introducing various issues and themes by way of a primer for further study. The chapter concludes with a brief discussion of several issues raised by eschatology, together with some advice on further reading and study.

The Kingdom of God

A kingdom motif is strongly evident in the Old Testament (henceforth OT). There are over three thousand references to kings, kingship, majesty and sovereigns. The OT also strongly emphasises the sovereignty of God, whether as creator, ruler or king, while majesty language is attributed to God (eg 1 Chron 29:11). In Judges the Israelites demanded a human king, in contrast to the existing theocracy where God was their king. Thus, the "God as King" motif runs strongly through the OT.

Meanwhile, a related aspect of major importance to the kingdom motif in the OT is the kingship of David. Note hope Matthew's genealogy (chapter 1) links Jesus with several pivotal characters and events in Israel's history, each separated by fourteen generations. Thus, the evangelist details fourteen generations between the patriarch Abraham and King David, a further fourteen generations separating King David from Israel's calamity (the exile), and finally another fourteen generations between the exile and the birth Jesus Christ. It is highly significant, particularly to the first century Jewish reader of Matthew's gospel, that the numerical value for David is 14 (each letter in the Hebrew alphabet has a numerical value; in Hebrew, David is spelled Dalet Vav Dalet, or DVD, that is, $4 + 6 + 4 = 16$). Thus, Matthew links Jesus with Israel's patriarch, Israel's greatest king and Israel's calamity, which would have been highly significant to his Jewish readership. But what is particularly important is this linking of Israel's King David with Jesus the Son of David. In 2 Samuel 7:12-17 God promises David through his descendant an everlasting throne and kingdom. It is ultimately Christ as Son of David, rather than David's son Solomon, through whom this prophecy is fulfilled. Thus, in the New Testament (henceforth NT) Nathaniel recognised Jesus as the King of Israel (John 1:49), the crowds on Palm Sunday praised Him as the King of Israel (John 12:14), while at His crucifixion they affixed a sign describing Him as king of the Jews (Matt 27:37), so that the chief priests mocked Him as the King of Israel (Matt 27:41-42).

Having identified the kingdom motif in the OT and tracing its development from King David through to Christ as the Son of David and King of Israel, we next move on to Jesus' teachings on the kingdom of God. Jesus commenced His ministry by proclaiming the imminent arrival of the kingdom of God (Mark 1:14-15). Yet elsewhere the NT seems to record the kingdom of God as an end times, or eschatological, event (eg Matt 13:47-50). Thus, we arrive at one of the first controversies surrounding eschatology. Some scholars (notably post-First World War scholar C.H. Dodd) argue that Jesus taught a "here and now" kingdom. We refer to this as "realised" or fulfilled eschatology (i.e. something that has already taken place). On the other hand, there are Christians (notably dispensationalists) who largely emphasise the "not yet" nature of the kingdom, that is, a futurist, as yet unfulfilled, eschatology. These dialectical understandings of the timing of the kingdom of God represent a major fault-line between rival groups within Christendom emphasising, on the one hand, a here and now, social gospel and/or church emphasis versus, on the other hand, an other-worldly, spiritual, not-of-this-world approach.

Both are problematic, in that both deny each other. Moreover, this artificial choice between the one or other very much follows a dialectical tendency that has underpinned Western culture and society since the Enlightenment. Fundamentally, it ignores how in first century Jewish-Christian minds there is no need for such an artificial choice, or the concept of holding opposites in tension so that both apply. As such, Evangelical scholars (for example, the late George Eldon Ladd, and more recently D.A. Carson) believe that both timings of the kingdom are simultaneously tenable, so that instead of speaking of a realised or future kingdom we can introduce a third term: the "inaugurated" kingdom of God, whereby we hold the "here and now" and "not yet" nature of the kingdom in tension.

Thus, Jesus came preaching and demonstrating the kingdom, inaugurating but not instituting it in its fullness. He ushered in the kingdom, giving us a glimpse of what the kingdom would look like. So, for example, in

Matthew's special miracle section (chapters 8 and 9), a section of that gospel that demonstrates the nature of the kingdom, Jesus demonstrated His (and by extension the kingdom's) power over illness (for example, the healing of a leper, the centurion's servant, Peter's mother-in-law); the kingdom's power over marginalisation (inclusion of a leper back into Jewish society, the woman with the haemorrhage, the calling of a tax collector); power over sin (Matt 9:1-8), the cosmic nature of the kingdom, demonstrated in Jesus' power over nature (Matt 8:23-7 cf the Messianic passage of Isa 11:6-9), the kingdom's power over oppression and Satan's kingdom (Matt 8:16, Matt 8:28ff cf Matt 12:22-28, note also Luke 11:20); and finally, the kingdom's power over death (bringing back to life the synagogue official's daughter). To recap then, whereas the kingdom of Satan resulted in pain, suffering, misery, exclusion and marginalisation, oppression and death, Jesus inaugurated the kingdom of God, and through His ministry and miracles provided us with an insight into what the kingdom will look like when it is instituted in its eschatological fullness, bringing healing, restoration, joy, inclusion, freedom from oppression, and ultimately life.

To summarise, despite this demonstration, this glimpse, of the kingdom, it has yet to be implemented in full. Jesus first had to come as Isaiah's Suffering Servant (Isaiah 53) before He returns as Coming King, about which the Bible has so much to say, and which—ultimately—is the culmination of the Bible story, when Christ returns literally and puts right all wrongs. This is the great eschatological hope of the Church.

As such, it is misleading, even unfortunate, when some Christians regard the cross as the culmination (or near culmination) of all things, almost as if when Jesus uttered on the cross, "It is finished" (John 19:30) God's work on earth was completed, salvation had come, and that is the end of the story. But how can that be the fulfilment of all things? Yes, Christ's work on earth was finished and the Christological aspect of God's salvific work was accomplished. But that is by no means the end of the divine plan. As we look around and see the desperate situation humanity and the world as a whole find themselves in, it is indeed depressing to say "this is it", that God has accomplished everything. By all means, let us recognise Christ's ministry and sacrifice in the context of the individual it saves, but it is essential that we also do not lose sight of the cosmic effects of Calvary and the events which are yet to occur, how the kingdom will be instituted in its fullness when Christ returns as Coming King. In his very useful *The God of Israel and Christian Theology* (1996) R. Kendall Soulen discusses the downplaying, or relegation of God as consummator of the age at the *eschaton*. Thus, believers should not view the cross as the zenith, or climax of God's work. Rather, it is a means to an end, not an end in itself. The cross brings about what God planned from the foundations of time (despite Adam's sin): God and man in perpetual communion finally brought about at the consummation of the age.

Systematising Eschatology
Given how entire books have been devoted to the subject of eschatology, it is clear that in the space remaining it would be impossible to describe in any satisfactory manner, much less analyse and discuss in depth, the various different approaches to eschatology, together with their merits and downfalls. Rather, the aim of this section is much less assuming or ambitious, primarily aimed at setting out some basic pointers and introducing in the broadest possible terms several concepts, to provide the reader with a minimalist framework to serve as simple basis for further study. The final section then concludes by providing advice on further reading and study.

There are several ways of approaching eschatology and organising eschatological texts and data into a system. But before looking at these briefly, it is important to that we first differentiate between individual and general eschatology. The former is concerned, as its name indicates, with what happens to the individual following death and covers issues such as whether or not there is an intermediate state (for example, soul sleep, or purgatory), together with the final state (hell, several views on annihilationism, and so on). General eschatology is concerned with the wider issues of the timing and nature of the return of Christ. There is some overlap between the two, for example, arguably the final state, while relating to the individual, might be viewed more as general eschatology given that it deals with judgment. Nonetheless, it is important to make this distinction between the two areas of eschatology and to note that, for the purposes of this chapter, we are focusing on general eschatology and the return of Christ.

One approach to categorising general eschatology is based on different interpretations of the Book of Revelation and other prophetic writings, though biblical scholar Millard Erickson notes that "the system can also be applied to distinguish general views of eschatology" (Erickson 1996, 1160). Erickson goes on to summarise the four categories (futurist, preterist, historical and symbolic, or idealist) which, given his precise and succinct definitions, are replicated here in full:

1. The futuristic view holds that most of the events described are in the future. They will come to fulfillment at then close of the age, many of them probably clustered together.
2. The preterist view holds that the events described were taking place at the time of the writer. Since they were current for the writer, they are now in the past.
3. The historical view holds that the events described were in the future at the time of writing, but refer to matters destined to take place throughout the history of the church. Instead of looking solely to the future for their occurrence, we should also search for them within the pages of history and consider whether some of them may be coming to pass right now.
4. The symbolic or idealist view holds that the events described are not to be thought of in a time sequence

at all. They refer to truths that are timeless in nature, not to single historical occurrences. (Ibid, 1160-61)

Another way in which Evangelical Christians approach eschatology is to categorise views within a millenarian system of classification. This term comes from the Latin word "mille" meaning "thousand", and it is based on the thousand-year period (or millennium) which is the earthly reign of Christ as detailed in Revelation 20:1-6. Central to this discussion is when the millennium takes place, and there are three main views.

Premillennialism (and its adherents, known as premillennialists) states that the *parousia* (Christ's return, Second Coming) precedes the millennial period, hence the term premillennial. Thus, Christ returns to establish His literal earthly reign, which lasts for a thousand years. Immediately prior to the Second Coming premillennialists believe there will be a time of horror and misery lasting seven years, known as the Great Tribulation (for details see Matthew 24:21 and Revelation 2:22, 7:14, together with Mark 13:19; Luke 21:23 and Revelation 3:10 - these references are linked to other eschatological passages, which build upon the idea of an apocalyptic tribulation period).

Postmillennialism, on the other hand, argues that the *parousia* takes place after this thousand-year period. Moreover, it regards the millennial period (which may or may not be interpreted as a literal thousand-year period) as Christ's reign not so much in person but through the Church. Postmillennialism, then, sees the millennial period as one of great advances for the Church as it seeks to establish the kingdom of God on earth. Historically, in attempting to establish Christ's earthly kingdom, postmillennialists have sometimes sought to capture social and political institutions to further this aim and mission. At that stage, when the kingdom is ushered in by the Church, Christ returns.

The third position is amillennialism. Millard Erickson states:

> Literally, amillennialism is the idea that there will be no millennium, no earthly reign of Christ. The great final judgment will immediately follow the second coming and issue directly in the final states of the righteous and the wicked. (Ibid., 1218)

Beyond these broad systems of classification are further issues to consider, particularly within the premillennial scheme. These include the nature and timing of the Great Tribulation and the rapture, and here is where eschatology can become not only somewhat complicated, but also polemical and at times highly divisive. Different views on the timing of the rapture sometimes revolve around whether it is argued that Christians go through (or partially go through) the tribulation period or not. Pretribulationism maintains they do not and thus are raptured, or caught away, immediately before the seven-year Great Tribulation commences.

Many posttribulationists, on the other hand, believe the *parousia* takes place after this tribulation period, and thus the day of the Lord is a much shorter event than the seven-year scheme posited by pretribulationists. Yet within posttribulationism there are several variations, so that the former president of Dallas Theological Seminary and pretribulationist John F. Walvoord identified the emergence of four views: classic posttribulationism, semiclassic posttribulationism, futuristic posttribulationism and dispensational posttribulationism (Walvoord 1976, 16-19).

Aside from these views are several mediating positions on the timing of the rapture, for example midtribulationism, which as its name implies argues that the rapture occurs midway through the Great Tribulation. Another is the pre-Wrath view, which differentiates between Satan's wrath in the early part of the Great Tribulation and God's wrath following the breaking of the Sixth Seal in the Book of Revelation. Thus, it is maintained believers are raptured before God manifests His wrath. Yet another view is a partial rapture theory, or modified versions arguing for the rapture taking place in stages during the tribulation period.

There is one further important feature of premillennial eschatology that we ought to mention briefly. The majority of pretribulationists are dispensationalist, an eschatological system that derives its name from a Greek word meaning "stewardship" (in the context of managing the affairs of a household). Dispensationalists believe in a divine plan for the world that is divided into a series of dispensations, or economies. There is some disagreement over the exact number of dispensations, but most commonly postulated is seven, each ending in judgment. The current dispensation (from Christ's redemptive work at Calvary through to the rapture) is known as the Church age, which is regarded as a parenthetical deviation from God's dealings with His people, ethnic Israel. Thus, dispensationalists make a clear distinction between Israel and the Church. Dispensationalists owe their modern origins to the Brethren leader John Nelson Darby (1800-1882), who emphasised separation from the world until the time of God's judgment.

To complicate matters further, in recent years some scholars from a dispensational background (notably Dallas Theological Seminary's Darrell Bock) have reassessed and re-stated a revised version of this system that has become known as progressive dispensationalism. Progressive dispensationalists seeks to attend to some of the criticisms aimed at dispensationalism, but have been criticised by some strongly holding to a traditional dispensationalism.

Emerging Issues and Further Study

Having highlighted several ways in which eschatology is systematised, it is worth highlighting several issues the topic raises before moving on to consider how to go about further study. From our survey thus far, it is clear that eschatology, while representing a fundamental aspect of biblical revelation and Christian thought, nonetheless is a highly complex, even bewildering area of theology. Inevitably, this has led to eschatology becoming a deeply controversial and unnecessarily divisive topic in some circles, marked by heated debate and argument. At times, this has even resulted in positions on, for example, the timing of the rapture unfortunately becoming tests of orthodoxy. Too often, I have seen believers not only be quite willing to fall out with each other over such issues, but even go so far as to label their fellow Christians heretics for their views on the timing of the rapture.

Consequently, while some Christians are obsessed with studying and debating eschatology (seemingly almost at the expense of other theological areas), the complex nature of the topic and the polemics it sometimes causes has resulted in the opposite effect, whereby other believers choose to avoid the subject completely. Thus, Millard Erickson refers to the extremes of boith "eschatomania" and "eschatophobia" (1996, 1155). As demonstrated in the above discussion concerning the kingdom of God set out in the first part of this chapter, it is essential for believers not to fall into either of these extreme camps of either becoming totally obsessed with eschatology at the expense of other areas of theology, or avoiding it completely and thus missing out on the culmination of the canonical story, our great eschatological hope and its role in our proclamation of the Gospel.

Another important issue to consider is how one's eschatological views can have a major bearing on shaping one's worldview, which in turn can have an impact upon a Christian's approach to ministry, engagement with the world and social and political affairs. This is particularly the case surrounding views of the millennial period and the timing of the rapture. Pretribulationists, who believe the rapture can happen at any time, without warning, regard the return of Christ as *imminent*. Thus, pretribulational dispensationalism's focus on the imminent return of Christ and otherworldliness, led classical Pentecostalism (which largely embraced dispensational eschatology during its foundational period) during much of the twentieth century to disengage from social and political issues and espouse a form of apoliticism. Things can only get worse, it was argued, so why seek to change society at all, especially in light of an imminent rapture? Only Christ can change the world when he returns, so it makes far more sense to spend what precious time is left winning souls prior to Christ's second coming, rather than wasting efforts on social and political activity. Hence, Pentecostals throughout much of the last century largely devoted their energies to urgent, aggressive evangelism, winning souls for Christ before that great and terrible day comes.

On the other hand, posttribulationism generally views the *parousia* as *impending*, that is, there will be an indication beforehand of its arrival (almost like signposts along a road nearing its destination). This difference between an imminent and impending view of the *parousia* is particularly pronounced between premillennial pretribulationism and postmillennialism. Pretributionalism's emphasis on an imminent Second Coming, together with the apocalyptic end-times scenario it envisages, makes it essentially pessimistic in outlook. On the other hand, postmillennialism's social and political agenda, seeking to emulate the ethical utterances of the Old Testament Prophets, offers a prophetic outlook that calls for action and social change, and is therefore utopian in character. Immediately noticeable is a tension between both systems: one is apocalyptic, otherworldly, and concerned with a future Kingdom of God, while the other is prophetic, concerned with this world and society, and which focuses on a Kingdom of God here and now (usually established by the Church). This is not just a theological point for discussion. In war-torn Central America during the revolutionary period of the 1980s it had a practical outworking and consequences, resulting in a clash between other-worldly Pentecostals and this-worldly Christians wanting to build God's kingdom on earth. In a region where revolutionaries and conservative capitalists fought each other, religious groups espousing the "right kind" of eschatology were co-opted by one side or the other, and conversely those espousing the "wrong kind" of eschatology faced reprisals (for a detailed discussion of this social and political outworking of eschatology in Central America, see Smith, 2008).

Having discussed some of the issues arising out of eschatology, the remainder of this chapter sets out very briefly how the reader interested in the subject can move forward in their study and understanding of eschatology.

However tempting it may be to do so, before exploring any of the eschatological systems outlined above, or becoming involved in polemical debates surrounding the millennial period, the tribulation and rapture, a very important and necessary first step is to spend some time in the Bible in a bid to identify and understand passages that deal with the end times. This is a crucial exercise, allowing the reader to become familiar over time with the nature and language of the Bible's prophetic and apocalyptic literature.

One useful way of going about this task is, during the course of one's day-to-day Bible reading, to make a note of passages that seem to be referring to the end times. To be sure, the newcomer to eschatology will not immediately pick up on every passage that has an eschatological thrust. Some passages are not immediately obvious as eschatological in context. On the other hand, other biblical passages have both a "here and now" and also an eschatological context. A case in point is the book of Obadiah, where the prophet's discussion of a current event (a devastating plague of locusts that is consuming the land) serves as a basis for foretelling a similarly disastrous plague of locust-like creatures in the future, as discussed in Revelation 9. It is easy to focus on the contemporary event and miss the eschatological lesson. Yet the prophet's various references to "the day of the Lord" indicate that while Obadiah is concerned with a contemporary event, ultimately this serves as content for an eschatological event. It is only by regular reading of the Bible will the student of hermeneutics begin to see such nuances and recognise apocalyptic and prophetic literature for what it is.

During the course of such independent reading and note-taking, the new student of eschatology will also begin to pick up on eschatological terminology and how it is used in the biblical literature. Terms and phrases such as, "the day of the Lord", "in that day", "the nations", "I will", are commonplace and will eventually be recognised for what they are. Aside from such phrases, during the course of regular reading one begins to note how certain biblical theology themes also seem to be rooted in eschatology, for example, final judgment, God's dealings with the nations, and particularly Israel. The biblical theme of Israel is referred or alluded to some three thousand times in the pages of Scripture, but especially noteworthy is how the culmination of the canonical narrative inextricably intertwines God's dealings with His people Israel with the end times. Thus, the two go hand in hand, and to relegate the one downplays the other. It is not insignificant that churches that downplay Israel likewise downplay eschatology, and vice versa.

Next, the reader should try to examine carefully the various prophecies identified in the above exercise and then seek to reach some conclusions as to whether they have been fulfilled or not. Bear in mind how the Bible sometimes indicates the concept of partial or multiple fulfilments of prophecy, which represents a key issue in deciphering some biblical prophecy. Certainly, the "abomination of desolation" theme finds several expressions throughout history, whether Antiochus Epiphanes' desecration of the Jewish temple as foretold by Daniel (9:27), Titus' destruction of the temple in AD 70 or an eschatological fulfilment, as discussed in Jesus' Great Eschatological Discourse in Matthew 24 and 25.

After spending some time reading the Bible and identifying eschatological texts, an important next stage is to move on to some reading about the nature and rules of interpreting prophetic and apocalyptic literature. A very helpful book in this regard is *How To Read the Bible For All*

Its Worth, by Gordon Fee and Douglas Stuart (2004). Such an emphasis upon understanding the hermeneutical rules for each type of biblical literature, or genre, represents a fundamental aspect of biblical interpretation, and in the case of apocalyptic literature it is crucial. To read prophetic or apocalyptic literature as, say, historical narrative or poetry, will inevitably result in misinterpretation of the passages, which is why knowing the hermeneutical rules for engaging with such writings is so important. For those interested in exploring how to interpret the different employed by the Bible authors in greater depth, another important book is Grant Osborne's *The Hermeneutical Spiral* (1991).

After all this personal study, the final stage in developing one's knowledge and understanding of eschatology is to begin engaging with the literature. Initially, it is advisable to avoid reading too much popular literature on the topic, which tends to be either unlearned, overly-polemical or simply aimed at selling books (eschatology is a great book seller). Instead, focus on more scholarly Evangelical treatments, ideally beginning with Millard Erickson's detailed treatment across various chapters in his excellent *Christian Theology* (1996). Erickson's approach is particularly useful in that it provides readers with a survey of different opinions, together with a valuable list of further reading, which is objective and seeks to avoid polemics. To be sure, Erickson reaches personal conclusions on some of the various issues he discusses, but the aim of his approach is to survey the various viewpoints and to discuss them fairly, even irenically. Erickson has also produced an entire volume devoted to the subject of eschatology (*A Basic Guide to Eschatology,* 1998) that will provide the student of eschatology with further scholarly treatment.

In conclusion, eschatology is a fundamental aspect of biblical studies and Christian thought. The end times represents the Church's great eschatological hope, the end of God's story—the Bible story—and thus deserves the attention of all serious students of the Bible.

References

Erickson, Millard (1996), *Christian Theology*. Grand Rapids, MI: Baker Academic.

Erickson, Millard (1998), *A Basic Guide to Eschatology: Making Sense of the Millennium*. Grand Rapids, MI: Baker Books.

Fee, Gordon and Stuart, Douglas (1994, REV 2004), *How To Read the Bible for All Its Worth*. Bletchley: Scripture Union.

Osborne, Grant (1991), *The Hermeneutical Spiral: A Comprehensive Introduction to Biblical Interpretation*. Downers Grove, IL: InterVarsity Press.

Smith, Calvin L. (2008), "Revolution and Revivalists: Pentecostal Eschatology, Politics and the Nicaraguan Revolution" in *Pneuma: Journal of the Society for Pentecostal Studies* 30, 55-82.

Souklen, R. Kendal (1996), *The God of Israel and Christian Theology*. Minneapolis, MN: Fortress Press.

Walvoord, John F. (1976), *The Blessed Hope and the Tribulation*. Grand Rapids, MI: Zondervan.

CHAPTER 8

Bible Polemics

DAVID L. WILLIAMS

The notion that objective truth can be known is much maligned within contemporary Western culture. Likewise the belief that Christians can and should pursue Biblical truth is regularly rejected, often in favour of an experience-based spirituality. Consequently errors and confusion creep at the margins of biblical faith and belief, whilst Jude's imperative that the church should "contend for the faith" (Jude 1:3) is dismissed as a disruptive, bickering over doctrinal minutiae. This is most apparent, understandably so, when highly contentious and polemical issues arise. This chapter will make the case that engaging in discussion of polemical issues should be viewed not as divisive, but rather as a thoroughly necessary means of addressing errors and confusion.

The initial task is to define precisely what is meant by biblical polemics, as some confusion and lack of clarity often exists over the precise meaning of this term, not least on account of the very similar but distinct field of theology known as apologetics. The definition of polemics suitably clarified, will lead into a brief discussion of the maligning of the pursuit of truth as a worthwhile activity, concluding that Christians must engage in controversial issues with the aim of upholding Scriptural values and biblical truths.

There are several New Testament examples of Jesus and the apostles engaging in what appears to be highly polemical engagements with opponents. The Christian church was born in a situation of doctrinal struggles, and so there are also countless examples from church history of the employment of highly polemical language in doctrinal debates. What are we to make of this? This question will also be addressed in a short section, as a preliminary to the final section, which answers the practical question: "How should Christians engage in polemics?" This chapter should thus harmonise with and complete the previous chapters, encouraging gently those who have now read this book with the confidence that their studies afford them the basic awareness to engage in modern controversies facing the church.

Defining Polemics in the Light of Apologetics

The nineteenth century liberal theologian Friedrich Schleiermacher employed a threefold categorisation of Christian theology: philosophical theology, historical theology and practical theology. He further divides philosophical theology into two subcategories: polemics and apologetics (Schleiermacher 1850, 105). Schleiermacher's categorisation is useful in bringing into focus the distinction between apologetics and polemics. In its simplest form apologetics is the defence of the Christian faith. The term derives from the Greek ἀπολογία (apologia), which may be defined as "a verbal defense, a speech defence" (Vine 1996, 29). It was originally used of a speech or an answer given as a reply. For example, in ancient Athens it referred to a courtroom response as part of the normal judicial procedure. After the accusation, the defendant was allowed to refute the charges with a defence or reply (apologia). The accused would attempt to "speak away" (apo—away, logia—speech) the accusation. From a theological perspective, apologetics is the defence of Christian truths in an attempt, to "speak away" external opposition and accusations against the faith.

For Frederic Howe, "the work of apologetics involves the careful study of and response to systems of interpreting reality which are opposed to the Christian Trinitarian system" (Howe 1978, 303), whilst Benjamin Warfield provides the definition:

Apologetics undertakes not the defence, not even the vindication, but the establishment, not, strictly speaking, of Christianity, but rather of that knowledge of God which Christianity professes to embody and seeks to make explicit. It may of course enter into defence and vindication when in the prosecution of its task it meets with opposing points of view and requires to establish its own standpoint or conclusions. (Warfield 1949, 233)

Apologetics then is an engagement in defence of the Christian faith, in its totality, in its substance and its presuppositions against all opposition. In short it is a reasoned defence against all external opposing ideologies.

What then is biblical polemics and how does it differ from apologetics? The English word *polemic* was derived, in the mid-17th century, from the French *polemique*. It referred to a type of hostile attack on someone else's ideas. In turn, *polemique* also traces back to the Greek word *polemikos*, which means "warlike" or "hostile", and is related to the noun *polemos*, meaning "war." The Merriam-Webster dictionary defines the term as

An aggressive attack on or refutation of the opinions or principles of another; the art or practice of disputation or controversy. (1995)

The American Heritage Dictionary of the English Language defines the term in a similar manner, appending its definition with the proposition that polemics is, "The practice of theological controversy to refute errors of doctrine" (2011).

Clarence Beckwith suggests that in theological usage, biblical polemics is

that department of theology which is concerned with the history of controversies maintained within or by the Christian Church, and with the conducting of such controversies in defense of doctrines held to be essential to Christian truth or in support of distinctive denominational tenets. (1953,109)

Note here, how Beckwith's definition employs the idea of controversies and disputes internal to the Christian Church. This is the crucial distinction between apologetics and biblical polemics. Apologetics is the engagement of the outsider with the aim of defending, for example, belief in the death and resurrection of Jesus or the authority of the Bible as the word of God. By contrast, polemics is an engagement within the church in matters of doctrinal debate.

Yet, whilst Beckwith's definition is perfectly valid, there is a broader consideration too. Beckwith's definition focuses upon, and is limited to, disputes over the essential doctrines of Christian truth, and whilst debates over these central doctrines of the Christian faith are vital, biblical polemics also includes an engagement with secondary or non-essential doctrines. For example, whilst conceding that some Christians may deem as central such topics as spiritual gifts, women in ministry, ecumenism, God's foreknowledge and man's freewill, in reality these are matters that Christians can and do hold different positions upon. Yet, correctly speaking, such matters should also fall under the category of biblical polemics.

Is The Pursuit Of Truth A Worthwhile Activity?
Given the above dictionary definitions, it is no surprise that biblical polemics has become both uncommon and unpopular in Christian circles. Most people understandably seek to avoid "hostile attacks", "warlike" contentions, "aggressive refutations", "disputations" and "controversies". Christians generally are more amenable to the apologetic task, with its inherent aim of defending a belief system and its hope of persuading the non-believer of the truth claims of a loving God manifest in the atoning sacrifice of His son Jesus Christ. Most well-read Christians could likely reel off a list of names, and perhaps have even read the works, of great Christian apologists; for example,

Augustine of Hippo, Justin Martyr, Thomas Aquinas, G K Chesterton, C S Lewis and more contemporary and popular figures such as Ravi Zacharias, Lee Strobel and William Lane Craig. Yet how many Christians have heard of Irenaeus of Lyons or have read in his multi-volumed "Against Heresies" about his doctrinal disputes with various Gnostic groupings? Certainly it is startling to discover, for example, that the eminent twentieth century theologian Benjamin Warfield held the position entitled the 'Chair of Didactic and Polemical Theology" at Princeton University from 1887 until his death in 1921. In 1943, just over twenty years after Warfield's death, "Apologetics and Polemics" was still a required course at Princeton. By the following year these courses were not even offered as electives. Michael Horton comments:

> Warfield was an example of what has become a dying breed in this century: a defender of truth at all costs, regardless of its unpopularity with either liberals or conservatives. (1996, 4)

Horton continues his assessment, pointing out

> There was a time, of course, when every theologian, whether Protestant or Roman Catholic, was a polemicist. Later, polemics became merely a distinct position on a theological faculty. Finally, it disappeared altogether in a spirit of tolerance. (Ibid, 5)

Whilst polemics and doctrinal debates may have now fallen from fashion, careful analysis of the New Testament texts would reveal that the formation and establishment of the Christian church occurred in a milieu of polemical doctrinal controversy. For example, in his epistle to the Galatians, Paul takes a strong approach in his response to the highly contentious and divisive issue of whether the Galatian believers were obligated to follow the Mosaic Law (Galatians 3). Elsewhere Paul addresses frankly the

Corinthian disputes over the use or non-use of foods sacrificed to idols (1 Cor 8), spiritual gifts (1 Cor 12), the role of women (1 Cor 14:33-36), and marriage and celibacy (1 Cor 7). Subsequent to the apostolic period, the fourth century Nicene Creed emerged out of a period of highly inflamed doctrinal conflict, largely related to a defence of orthodoxy in the Arian controversy, in which Arius (c. AD 250-336) propounded distinctly unorthodox views regarding the incarnation of Christ. Likewise, the Protestant Reformation can be viewed as a polemical attempt by the reformers to engage in refutations of the doctrinal errors of the Catholic Church. Martin Luther's famous allegations, at the Diet of Worms in 1521, that the Pope and the council had fallen into error and glaring inconsistency is a prime example of such an attempt.

In a similar manner, J Gresham Machen, the early twentieth century Professor of New Testament at Princeton University, urged a return to the importance of a scholarly and biblical defence of the Christian faith within the Church, making the point that

> In the first place, it should be directed not only against the opponents outside the Church but also against the opponents within. The opponents of Holy Scripture do not become less dangerous, but they become far more dangerous, when they are within ecclesiastical walls. (1996, 27)

Yet in surveying the contemporary church scene one is tempted to ask the question: What happened? From where did the notion arise that Christians should not refute doctrinal error within their midst, or engage in issues of serious dispute? Certainly the Church generally has shunned its capacity to discern truth from error. John MacArthur soberly reminds us that

> Discernment demands that we should hold biblical convictions with the most fervent tenacity. Titus 1:9 says a basic requirement for every elder is that he be

126

the kind of man who (holds) fast the faithful word which is in accordance with the teaching, that he may be able to exhort in sound doctrine and to refute those who contradict, or we do not fulfil our divine calling. (1994, 52)

Martin Lloyd Jones summed up the situation over three decades ago:

> Disapproval of polemics in the Christian Church is a very serious matter. But that is the attitude of the age in which we live. The prevailing idea today in many circles is not to bother about these things. As long as we are all Christians, anyhow, somehow, all is well. Do not let us argue about doctrine, let us all be Christians together and talk about the love of God. That is really the whole basis of ecumenicity. Unfortunately that same attitude is creeping into evangelical circles also and many say that we must not be too precise about these things. If you hold that view you are criticizing the Apostle Paul, you are saying that he was wrong, and at the same time you are criticizing the Scriptures. The Scriptures argue and debate and dispute; they are full of polemics. (1970, 113)

The very concept of holding fast to a faithful word or exhorting a fellow believer in sound doctrine rings quite foreign to the modern and postmodern ear. To hold fast and to exhort sound doctrine implies a definiteness and certainty of truth that implies an inherent value to doctrinal faith worth preserving. Yet we live in culturally and philosophically changeable times in which we have become accustomed to viewing all our philosophical and theological beliefs as being in a state of perpetual flux. The dominant metaphors of the late twentieth and early twenty-first century are evolution and revolution. Nothing remains the same as "a considerable measure of change occurs relatively quickly and with such all-encompassing breadth and depth that it becomes difficult to comprehend and absorb" (Williams 2016, 14). A concept of truth either changes with the times or it becomes outmoded and thus discarded by a throwaway society as "Traditions, social structures, ways of thinking and perhaps just as importantly the people who espouse such values become obsolete" (Ibid).

By contrast Jude affirms that the Christian faith is at its central core fundamentally stable and unchanging (Jude 1:3). Consequently the philosophical and theological revolutions may be rejected in favour of a thorough contending for the faith once delivered for all generations of believers (Ibid). This idea that truth is stable and unchanging, though foreign to the contemporary mind-set, is nevertheless prevalent throughout Scripture as pictured by Isaiah, who declares, "The grass withers, the flower fades; but the word of our God will stand forever" (Isaiah 40:8). God does not change and neither does His truth. Certainly our knowledge of Him and His truth is partial, yet insofar as it is knowledge, it is accurate and unchangeable. The implication is clear: if the Christian faith comprises a stable, unchanging, core truth then the general task of biblical polemics is obvious, namely that the Christian must engage in controversial issues with the view of upholding Scriptural values and Biblical truths.

"Disputations", "Refutations" and "War-Like" Language in Scripture and the Early Church

Robert Sproul remarks that Marcion of Sinope (c.85-c160 AD) was "the arch heretic of all time regarding biblical continuity" (2013, 16). Marcion was certainly denounced as such by the early church for holding the view that the God of the Old Testament was a spiteful and angry *demiurge*, in direct contrast to what he perceived as the loving God portrayed in the pages of the New Testament. Unsurprisingly, Marcion rejected the Old Testament and produced a much-truncated version of the New Testament. Marcion once met with Polycarp and asked him "Do you know me?" Polycarp answered, "I do know you. You are the firstborn of Satan." (Cited in Schaff 1867, 416). This is abrasive and shocking language to the modern mind, and, understandably, contemporary Christians largely avoid employing such colourful turns of phrase. Yet we must ask: Does such straight talk have any precedent in Scripture? There are some grounds for believing so. Certainly it is likely Paul was expressing a wish that the Galatian legalists, who advocated Gentile circumcision, would castrate themselves also (Gal. 5:12). Employing similarly striking language, Jesus informed the religious leaders of his day that they were little more than "white washed tombs" (Matt 23:27), a "den of robbers" (Matt 21:13) and "a brood of vipers.... who are evil" (Matt 12:34), accusing them of travelling over land and sea to evangelise one person only to make that individual more of a child of hell than themselves (Matt 23:15). Likewise John the Baptist lost his life on account of his polemical denunciation of Herod, who had taken and married Herodias, his brother Phillip's wife. Jesus also had a few sharp words to say about Herod (Luke 13:32) whilst also refusing to even speak to Herod when appearing before him (Luke 23:8). Several further examples from Scripture could be cited, and here the contemporary Christian begins to squirm as he is confronted with such abrasive speech. What should we make of this sort of inflammatory speech as a stylistic approach to polemical engagement?

The Christian must speak against the enemies of the faith, irrespective of whether they are located internally or externally. Sometimes the hard word must be spoken when it would be easier to speak a soft word, and there are times that the hard word is the godly word, even where it may appear to be harsh or divisive. Yet we must also speak the hard word in a manner that is communicative for the times in which we live, as a second century approach may not necessarily work in the twenty-first century. Marcionism remains very much a concern today, via for example the common "red letter", or "words of Jesus only" approach to the Bible, as often exemplified in the prevalent belief and teaching that God extends only love and tolerance, to the exclusion of any notion of judgment. Yet it would be foolhardy to dismiss the sort of folk who espouse such neo-Marcionite ideas as the "firstborn of Satan", not least because so few people would countenance a belief in Satan. Consequently, to be labelled as Satan's firstborn amounts to little more than rhetorical hyperbole and abuse, and to employ such terminology today would likely sound far worse than it did in the second century. By contrast, the rhetorical style of the early Church Fathers would have provided real impact; as the accusation of being the "firstborn of Satan" was taken seriously.

Nevertheless, though acknowledging the need for occasional straight talking, it is instructive to recall that whilst Jesus denounced the Pharisees in no uncertain terms, he would shortly thereafter give his life for them and for those who came under their influence. By telling the truth about the Pharisees and Herod, Jesus (and John the Baptist) demonstrated immense love for those who were tempted to follow these errant individuals. Likewise, Marcion was leading people away from, rather than towards, the true God and into what Irenaeus termed "an abyss of madness and blasphemy against Christ" (cited in Schaff 1867, 315). We should not think that Polycarp or Irenaeus or many others took any particular pleasure from attacking error, and careful reading of Irenaeus' "Against Heresies" would suggest that the entangled knot of gnostic heresies that he did address was, for him, a cumbersome task, as he called the errant to repentance through warnings and prayerfulness. Although the early Church Fathers engaged in a full-blooded battle for doctrinal purity, they nevertheless understood that the Church and her witness suffered whenever and wherever Christians disagreed.

Iain Murray takes up this theme, reflecting upon an encounter between D. M. Lloyd-Jones and T. T. Shields. Murray states that the Baptist leader (Shields) was sometimes too controversial, too denunciatory, and too censorious. Rather than helping young Christians by the strength of his polemics against liberal Protestants and Roman Catholics, Lloyd-Jones believed that Shields was losing the opportunity to influence those whose need is positive teaching. (1982, 271)

Yet Lloyd-Jones was himself no stranger to polemical discourse. Reference has already been made, above, to his regret at what he saw as the diminishing of the polemical task. He also clashed quite publicly with John Stott over the question of whether evangelicals should remain within the established Church of England. In spite of this, and revealing something of his pastoral inclination, Lloyd-Jones insisted that polemics should not comprise a major thrust of Christian ministry. Shields had considered himself to be following in the footsteps of Paul who had confronted Peter (Gal 2:11-13). Lloyd-Jones responded

The effect of what Paul did was to *win* Peter round to his position and make him call him 'our beloved brother Paul' (2 Peter 3:15). Can you say the same about the people whom you attack? (Ibid, 273)

This understanding can lead us back, full-circle, to consider the sort of rhetoric employed by the apostle Paul, who, when occasion demanded, not only denounced without reservation heresy and apostasy, but also did not hesitate to name the names of the guilty. Among these, for example, were "Hymenaeus and Philetus" who taught that the "resurrection is past" (2 Tim 2:17–19). Paul could on this occasion have taken the approach that truth will overcome error, and that consequently he could employ a pious and patient silence in response, yet he assures Timothy that "God's firm foundation stands" (2:19). No amount of erroneous teaching about the resurrection could subvert the reality of the resurrection, yet the effects were "upsetting the faith of some" (2:18). Paul was aware that the errors of Hymenaeus and Philetus could "spread like gangrene" (2:17). And here is the key issue: Paul warns Timothy sharply, and names the names of those who propagate error, not primarily for the sake of prevailing in polemical engagement, but for the welfare of human souls.

Yet, in spite of the occasions when Christians must engage with a difficult word, in confrontation of core gospel issues, there are also many secondary issues upon which Bible-believing Christians genuinely differ. For example, there has been much, often heated debate in the past thirty to forty years on the question of whether Christian worship should take a traditional or contemporary nature? Should theology or musical style drive the church's worship as it meets to celebrate its saviour? What position should the church take on the charismatic gifts and developments in the global charismatic movement? Are these gifts for today or did they cease functioning in the apostolic period? The question remains: how should Christians practically engage in polemics?

How Should Christians Engage in Polemical Disputes?

One approach to this question would be to mimic that employed by the authors of the Nicene Creed; namely to construct statements of faith that reflect the core doctrines of the Christian faith. Christians may then repetitively repeat these credal statements. Yet to do so is hardly a polemic against ether serious doctrinal error or an engagement with secondary issues. To make credal statements is certainly a reasonable starting point but there is a clear requirement for strongly supportive scriptural arguments that address error. To attempt to refute a modern day Arius by simply affirming, via the Nicene Creed, the pre-existent deity of Christ, who was "begotten not made", will not likely gain much traction with today's Arius, and surely one of the prime aims of polemics is to persuade Arius to change his mind. How may this be achieved?

The apostle Paul provides some clues in his first letter to Timothy, where he implores the young pastor to keep a close watch on himself and to his doctrine, to persist in it and so to save both himself and those who hear him (1 Tim 4:16). Essentially Paul's command to Timothy comprises two broad components: firstly, Timothy was personally to be an "example in speech, in conduct, in love, in faith, in purity" (1 Tim 4:12); that is, his behaviour and his attitudes towards other believers had to be exemplary and it is these that serve as the foundation for how and what he should speak. Secondly, he was to pay close attention to his doctrine, to "devote (himself) to the public reading of Scripture, to exhortation, to teaching" (2 Tim 4:14) for in so doing he would prove himself "a good servant of Christ Jesus, being trained in the words of faith and of the good doctrine that (he has) followed" (1 Tim 4:6). Furthermore he should "have nothing to do with irreverent, silly myths" (I Tim 4:7).

Paul's command here is paralleled in his subsequent communication with Timothy where he offers an unequivocal warning that followers of Christ should avoid "foolish and ignorant disputes" as these produce nothing but conflict. Disciples of Jesus are not to be quarrelsome should not engage in pointless disputes, but on the contrary must evidence gentleness, patience and a capacity to teach. Paul makes the reason for this manifestly clear, specifically that the aim of all correction and polemical engagement is that those who are in opposition may be granted repentance by God, coming to knowledge of the truth and escaping error (2 Tim 2:23-26). These are unequivocal commands of Scripture and the Christian who ignores them does so at his or her peril. Note here that Paul is specifically referring to how the "servant of the Lord" should behave, the clear implication being that those who disobey disqualify themselves from being considered as God's servants. This is a serious situation and Paul lists four essential aspects that are worthy of further consideration here.

First, the servant of the Lord is to be gentle. The Greek word ἤπιος (épios) means gentle or mild and is related to the term that Paul utilises in the description of his attitude to the Thessalonians: "but we were gentle (Gk: ἤπιοι [ēpioi]) among you, just as a nursing mother cherishes her own children" (1 Thes 2:7). The word picture here is clear, namely that in polemical engagement the servant of the Lord is to approach others with the type of gentleness that a mother displays towards her baby. James, in his epistle, echoes this idea, warning his readers against earthly and unspiritual selfish ambition and jealousy, pointing out that the "wisdom from above is first pure, then peaceable, gentle (Gk: ἔπειτα [epieikēs]), open to reason" (James 3:13-18). Second, the servant of the Lord is to exhibit patience (Gk: ἀνεξίκακος [anexikakos]); that is, a capacity to forbear and to endure. Nigel Turner suggests that the term demonstrates "the quality of patiently affirming a belief in the face of mockery (Wis 2:19)" (1997, 321). This suggests that in dealing with error an attitude of patience should characterise all polemical engagement irrespective of the tone that is employed against the polemicist. Third, is a characteristic of gentle humility or considerate meekness (Gk: πραΰτης [prauté]). Such a quality is a divinely bestowed virtue, a fruit of the Spirit listed in Galatians 5:23. This suggests that those who struggle and strive in their own flesh, demonstrating contentiousness and antagonism do so from false and ungodly motives. Likewise in his first epistle, Peter instructs his readers that having honoured Christ as Lord they should be perpetually prepared to make a defence (Gk: ἀπολογίαν [apologian]) for the hope that is within them, but to do so with gentleness (Gk: πραΰτητος [prautētos]) and respect. Interestingly here the quality of gentleness is intimately linked with the root word that provides definition to the entire apologetic task.

Beyond these attitudinal qualities Paul also expects the servant of the Lord to have the capacity or aptitude to teach (Gk: διδακτικός [didaktikos]) the word of God. Paul again utilises this term in his first letter to Timothy, where he sets out the requirements for church overseers or bishops. Amongst several other stellar qualities a church leader must also have the aptitude to teach God's word. (1 Tim 3:2). How is this capacity acquired? Again Paul provides Timothy with the strong advice that he should "do his best" (Gk: σπουδάζω" [spoudazó] - make haste, give due diligence, "study" (KJV) or "work hard" (NLT)). What is the reason for this effort? That Timothy would be able to present himself to God as a worker who can correctly handle Scripture (2 Tim 2:15). This, in essence, is the exegetical task that underlies the polemical task, the capacity and willingness to study Scripture, to know it and to understand it such that the correct handling of God's word is manifest in any situation.

Returning to 1 Tim 3:2, the requirement for a leader to have an aptitude to teach should immediately remind us that polemical debate should occur most naturally within the context of ecclesiastical discipleship. Consequently, anyone who is not involved, or unwilling to be involved, in a local church of some description, precludes themselves from involvement in the polemical task. Certainly care should be exercised when encountering the solitary, unaccountable Christian who sets himself up as a type of "watchman" for the church at large. This is not to say that biblical polemics may not be carried out with and amongst those outside of a believer's immediate ecclesiological circle, but that commitment to such a body of believers is nevertheless a requirement. The reason should be manifestly obvious, namely that the daily and weekly interaction with other believers should engender within the polemicist a humble dependence upon Christ who will not only produce the sanctifying work of the Spirit in the life of the teacher but also will ensure that biblical polemics do not become reduced to the level of the theoretical, the purely academic or a highly personal attack on other believers. Certainly Christ's Great Commission to the Church is not that his followers would win arguments, but that they would teach and make disciples, clearly defining truth for those who seek to be fellow disciples of

Christ (Matt 28:19-20). Thus when polemical debates are entered into within the context of the local church, it should be tempered with love and the objective of protecting the flock. Paul makes this abundantly clear in his powerful discourse on love (1 Cor 13), pointing out that to do otherwise reduces the impact of truthful speech to little more than a "noisy gong or a clanging cymbal" (13:1). Note however that Paul's discussion of love is both preceded and succeeded by discussion of the contentious issue of spiritual gifts; the point being that it is in the very context of addressing polemical issues that Paul underlies the necessity of correct attitudes.

Conclusion

Claims that objective truth can be known are much maligned within contemporary society, as much so within the church as outside. Further, where the existence of truth is acknowledged, the pursuit of it is customarily relegated to the category of unnecessary divisiveness. This is a serious issue for polemical discourse, to the point that biblical polemics have become so unfashionable that clear definition of the task has been necessary here. Having defined biblical polemics as a somewhat "warlike" engagement in controversial issues, the question raised must be: Is it worth pursuing truth with such tenacity? A condensed survey of selected examples from Jesus, Paul, the early church and more recent times would suggest that not only is the pursuit of truth worthwhile, it is an essential activity.

How, then, should Christians engage in biblical polemics? Paul, who reminded Timothy of two essential elements, supplies the answer: Firstly, the polemicist must display personal qualities of gentleness, patience and humility. Secondly, the polemicist must acquire a capacity to correctly handle God's word, via serious study of Scripture; that is, engagement in the exegetical task. When biblical polemics are approached in such a manner, and discourse is couched in the diction of gentle and reasonable interchange, biblical polemics should quickly lose its "warlike" and "controversial" edginess in favour of a gentle, wise capacity to engage in genuinely difficult matters.

References

Beckwith, C. A. (1953), "Polemics" in in P. Schaff, G. W. Gilmore, & S. M. Jackson, eds., *New Schaff-Herzog Encyclopedia Of Religious Knowledge* (Vol. IX). Grand Rapids, Michigan: Baker Book House.

Horton, M. S. (1996), "How To Be Polemical Without Being a Downright Nasty Person" in *Modern Reformation* , *5* (5), 4-9.

Howe, F. R. (1978), A Comparative Study of the Work of Apologetics and Evangelism. *Biblitheca Sacra 135* (540), 303-312.

Lloyd-Jones, D. M. (1970), *Romans: An Exposition of Chapters 3:20-4:25: Atonement and Justification.* Grand Rapids, MI: Zondervan Publishing House.

MacArthur, J. F. (1994), *Reckless Faith: When the Church Loses its Will to Discern.* Wheaton, IL: Crossway Books.

Machen, J. G. (1996), "Polemics: A Defense of Defending" in *Modern Reformation* 26-32 (Sept/Oct).

Murray, I. H. (1982), *D. Martyn Lloyd-Jones: The First Forty Years 1899-1939.* Edinburgh: The Banner Of Truth Trust.

Schaff, P. (1867), *Ante-Nicene Fathers* (Vol. 1). Grand Rapids, MI: Christian Classics Ethereal Library.

Schleiermacher, F. W. (1850 [Reprint 2007]), *Brief Outline of the Study of Theology, Drawn up to Serve as the Basis of Introductory Lectures.* (W. Farrer, Trans.) Eugene, OR: Wipf and Stock Publishers.

Sproul, R. C. (2013), *How Then Shall We Worship?* Colorado Springs, CO: David C Cook.

The American Heritage Dictionary of the English Language 5th Edition ed. (2011), Boston, MA: Houghton Mifflin.

The Merriam Webster Dictionary 2nd Revised ed. (1995), Springfield, MA: Merriam Webster.

Turner, N. (1997), *Christian Words*. London: T&T Clark Publishers.

Vine, W. E. (1996), *Vine's Complete Expository Dictionary*. (M. F. Unger, & W. White, Eds.) Nashville: Thomas Nelson.

Warfield, B. B. (1949), "Apologetics" in P. Schaff, & S. M. Jackson, eds., *The New Schaff-Herzog Encyclopedia of Religious Knwoledge (Aachen - Basilians)* (Vol. 1). Grand Rapids, MI: Baker Book.

Williams, D. (2016). "Same-Sex Relationships: Final Frontier In The Cultural Revolution?" in *Evangelical Review of Theology and Politics* (May).

ABOUT THE CONTRIBUTORS

THOMAS FRETWELL holds B.Th. and M.A. degrees in Theology from the University of Chester. He is an associate tutor in Theology at King's Evangelical Divinity School (KEDS) and an associate speaker with Creation Ministries International.

WALTER LAMBERTI holds an M.A. in Theology from the University of Chester and is a tutor at KEDS. He is currently enrolled on a Ph.D. programme in Theology at Aberdeen University. He is a member the Society of Biblical Literature and the Evangelical Theological Society.

DONNA ORR earned a First Class Honours B.Th degree at the University of Wales, Trinity St David, and an M.A. (Theology) with distinction from the University of Chester. She is an associate tutor at KEDS and is also a librarian.

ANTHONY ROYLE holds a B.Th. degree from the University of Chester and is currently completing an M.A. in Theology. He is a tutor for the Knowing Your Bible and Jewish-Christians Studies programmes at KEDS.

CALVIN L. SMITH holds degrees in Education, History and Politics and a Ph.D. in Theology from the University of Birmingham. He is Principal of KEDS, edits the *Evangelical Review of Theology and Politics,* and publishes widely.

DAVID L. WILLIAMS holds a B.Th. (Hons) degree from the University of Wales, Lampeter, and an M.A. in Theology from the University of Chester. He is a tutor at KEDS, a member of the school's academic committee and director of the Knowing Your Bible programme.

MATTHEW WONG holds a DipHE in Biblical Hermeneutics and an M.A. (Theology) from the University of Chester. He also holds a B.A. (Hons) degree in Geography from the University of Nottingham. He is a tutor on the Knowing Your Bible programme at KEDS.